Coloring Book
Merry Christmas and Happy New Year

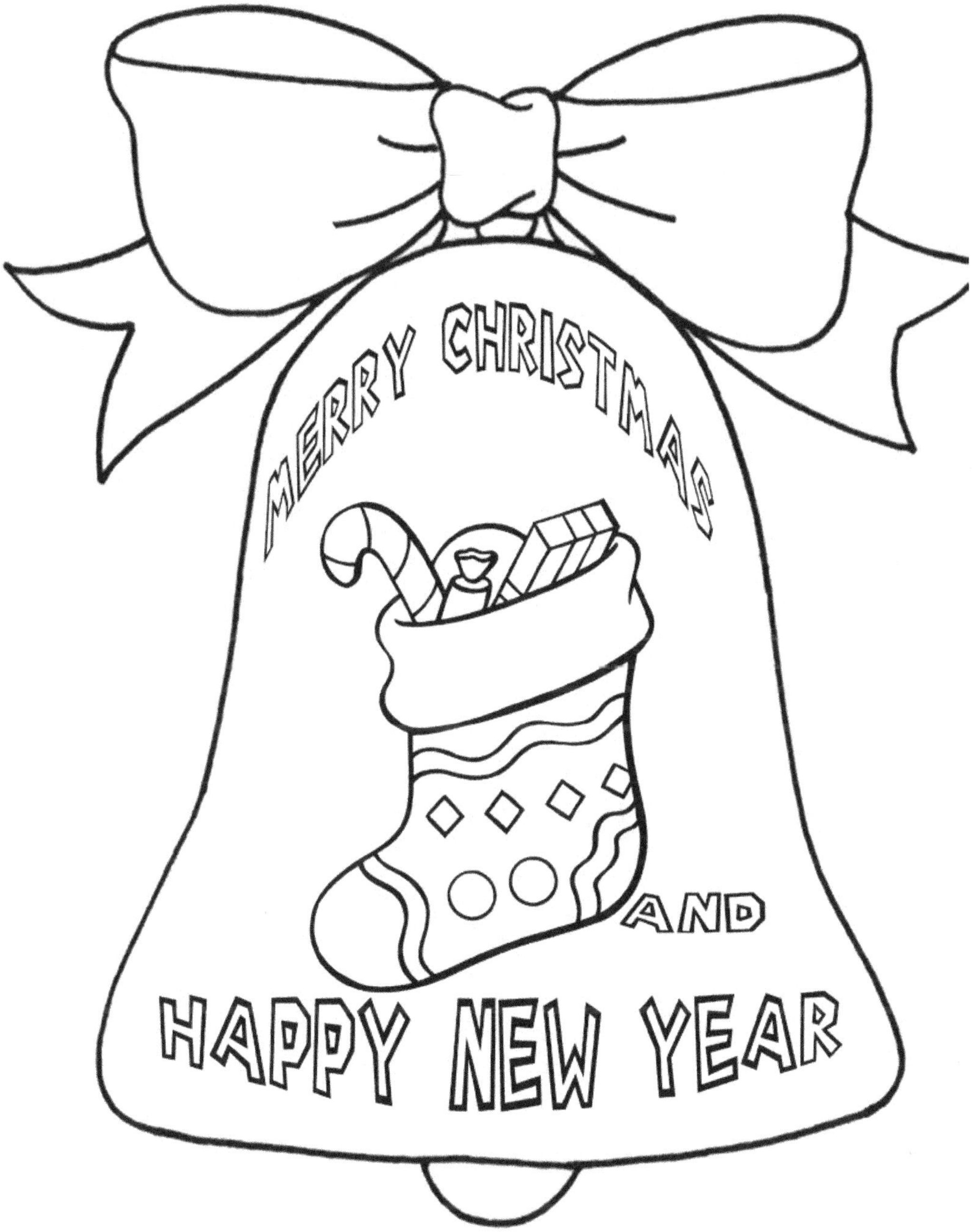

Patty Mario

Coloring Book

Merry Christmas And Happy New Year

Copyright: Published in the United States by **Patty Mario**
Published November 2017

All rights reserved. No part of this publication may be reproduced, stored in retrieval system, copied in any form or by any means, electronic, mechanical, photocopying, recording or otherwise transmitted without written permission from the publisher. Please do not participate in or encourage piracy of this material in any way. You must not circulate this book in any format Patty Mario *does not control or direct users' actions and is not responsible for the information or content shared, harm and/or actions of the book readers.*

ISBN-13: 978-1979865937

ISBN-10: 1979865930

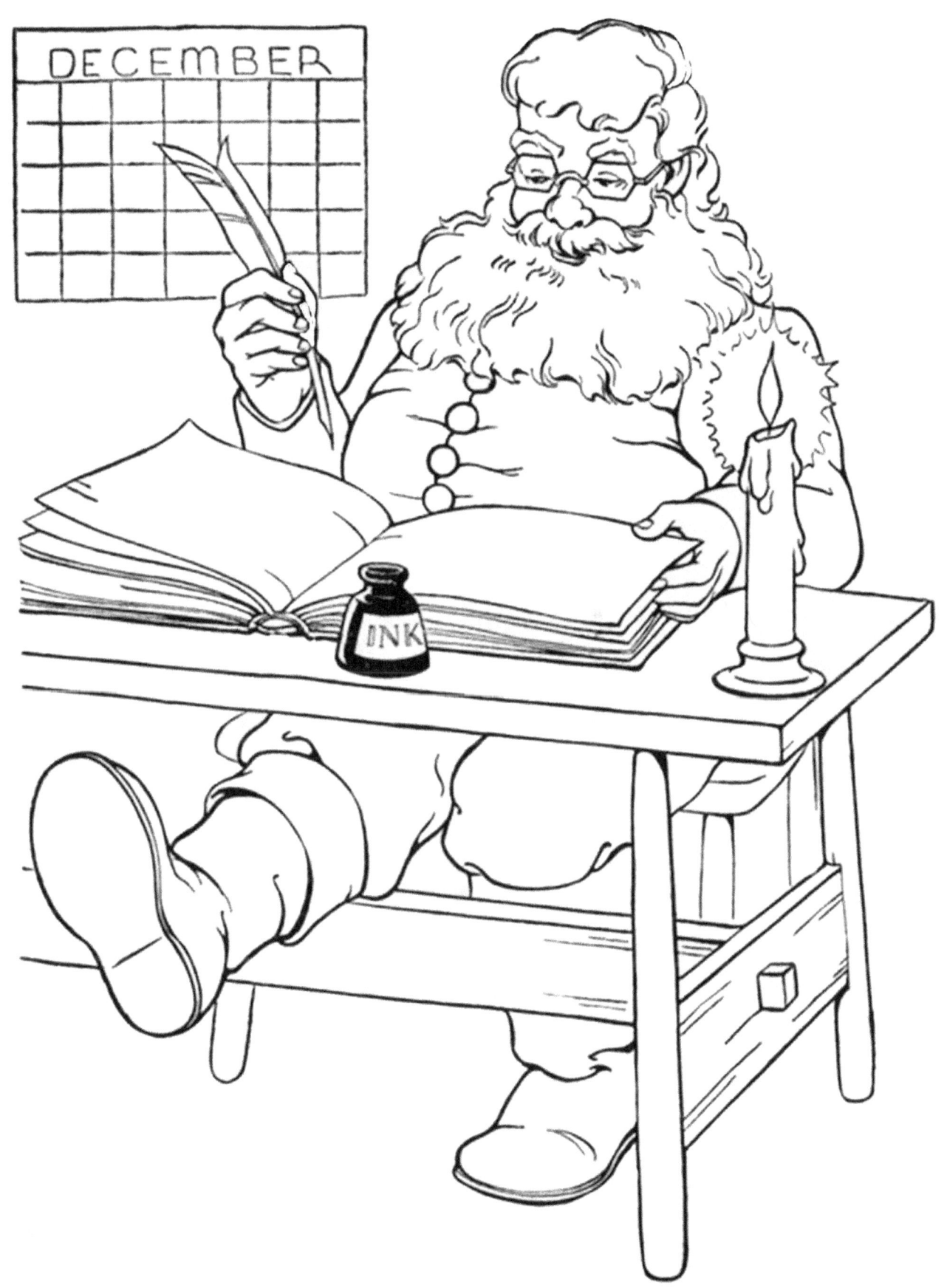

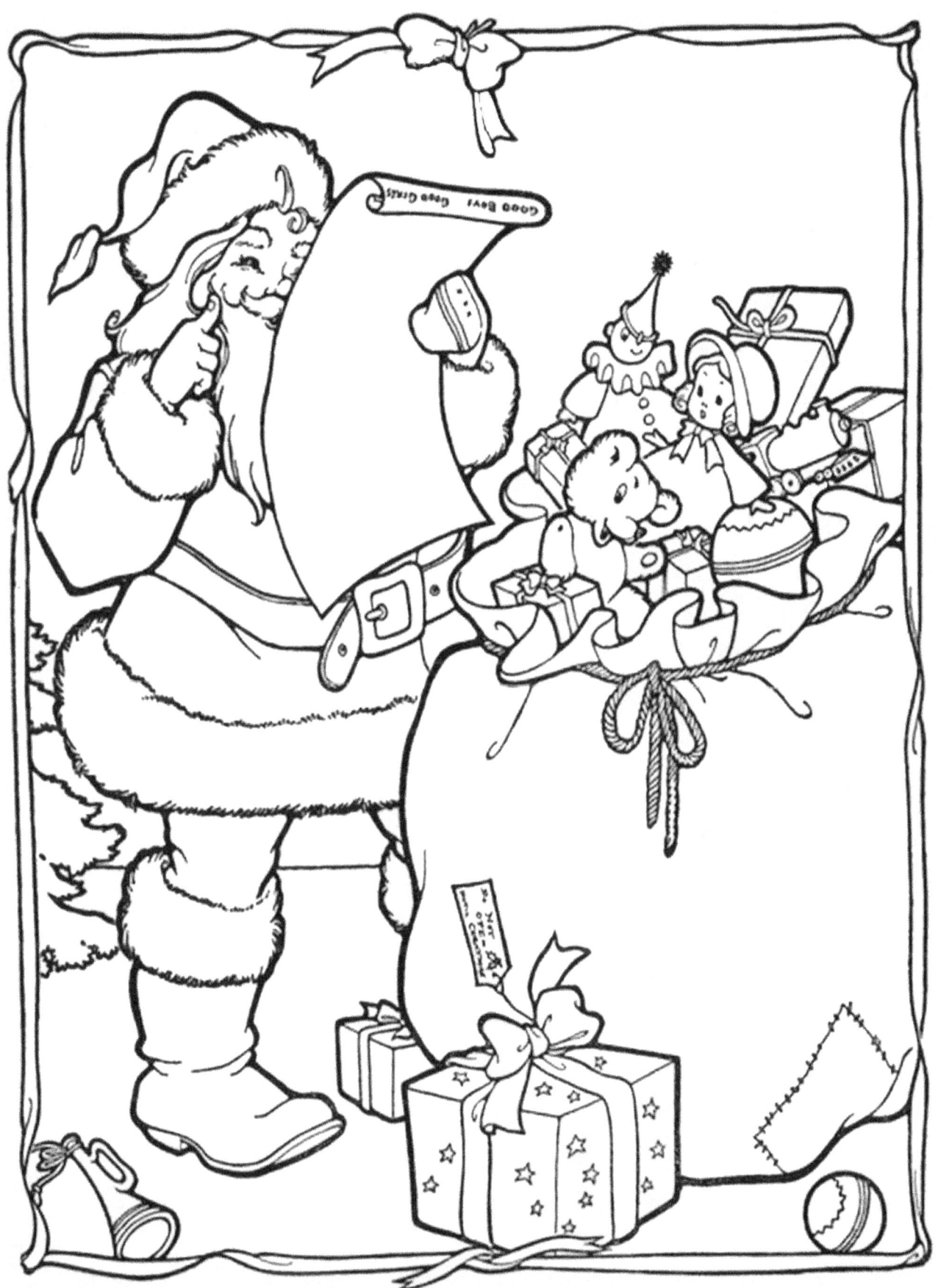

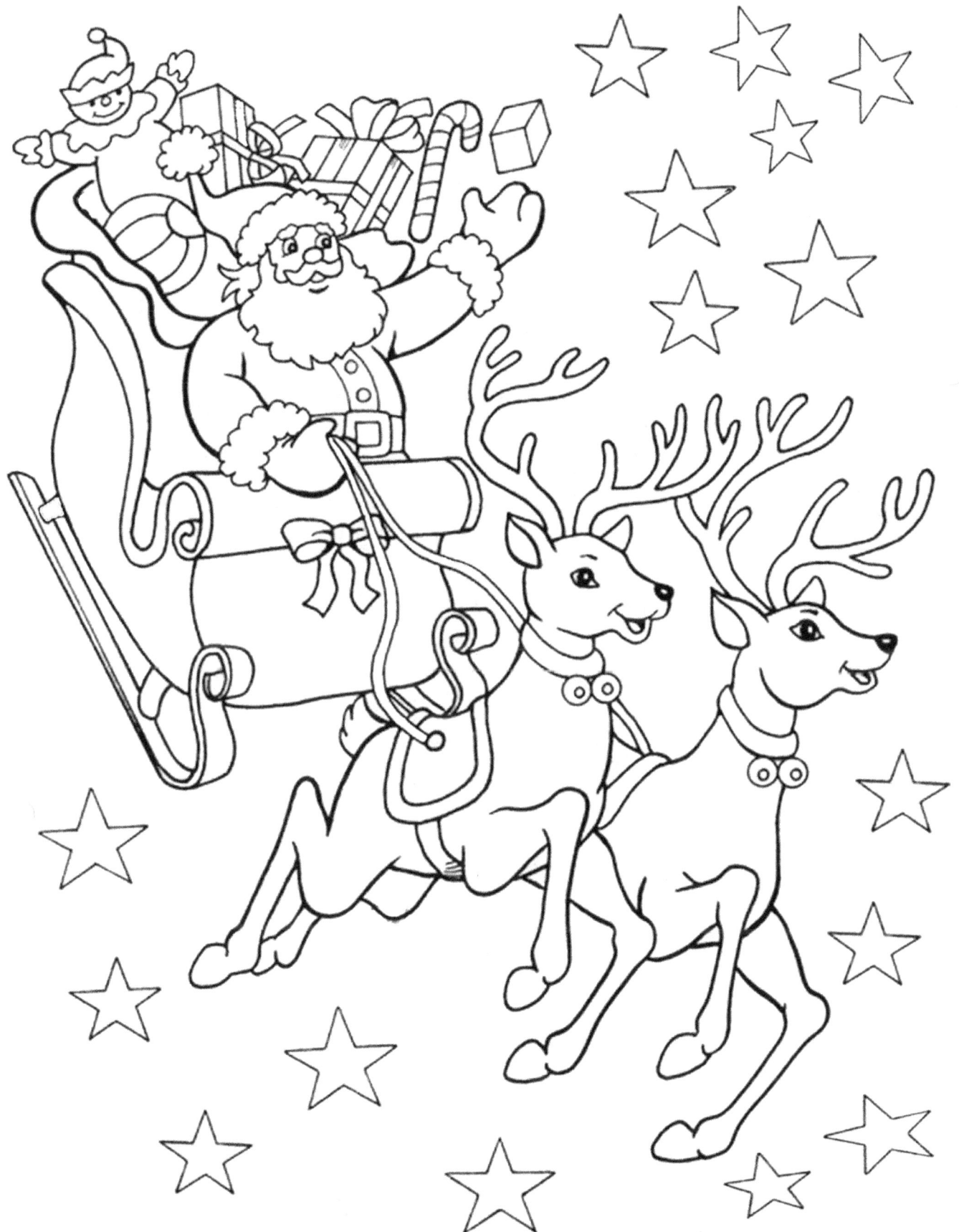

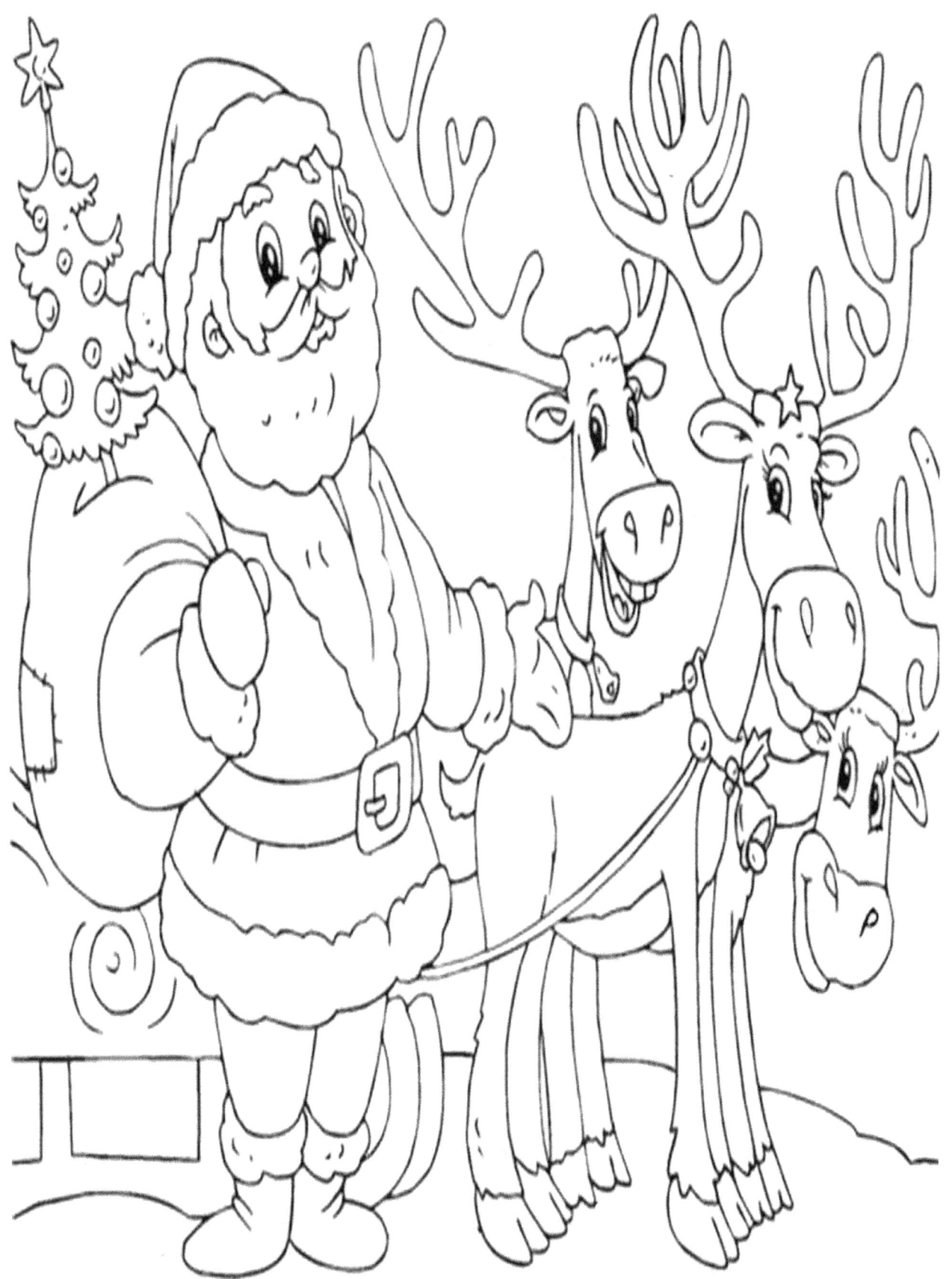

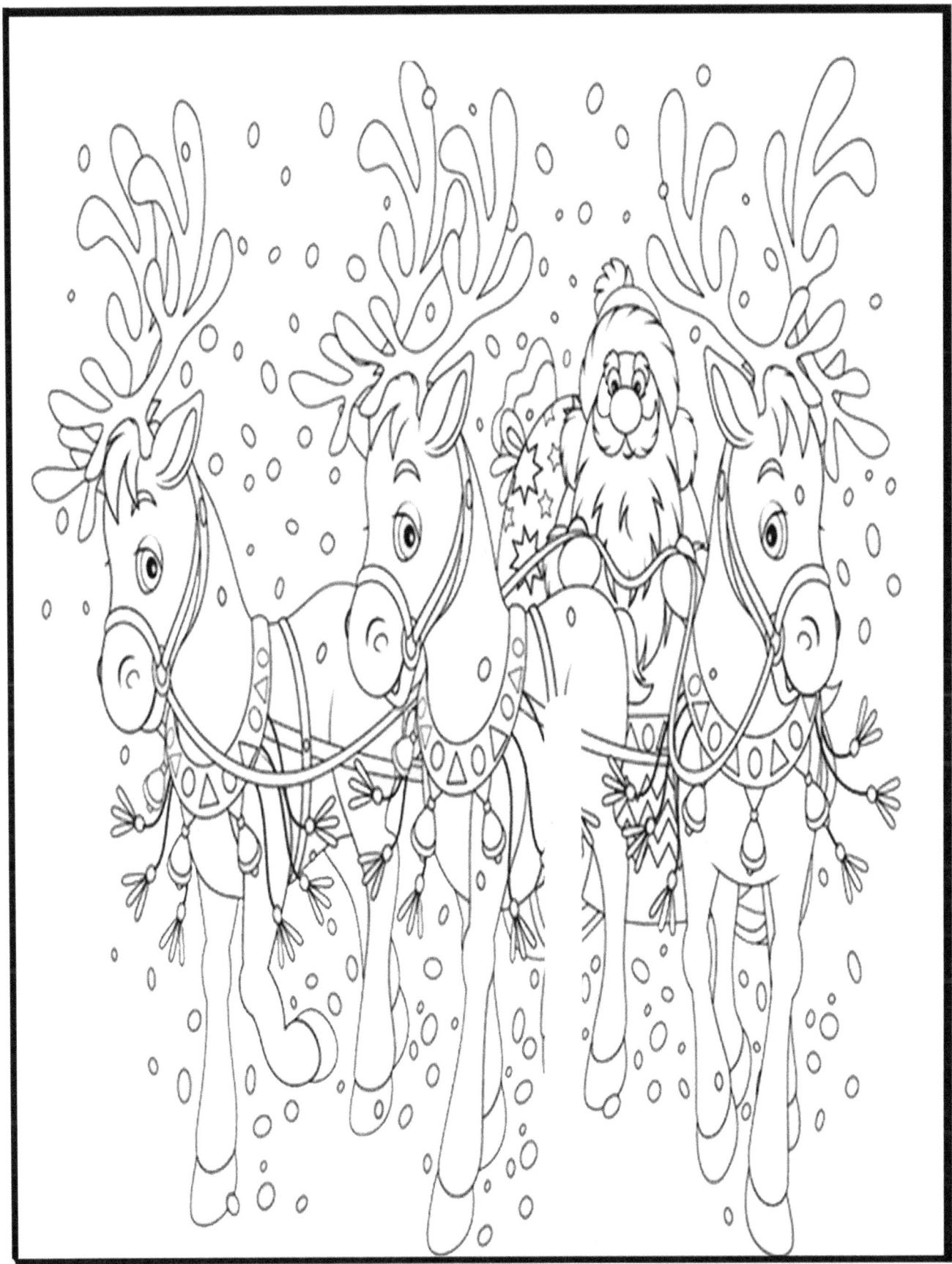

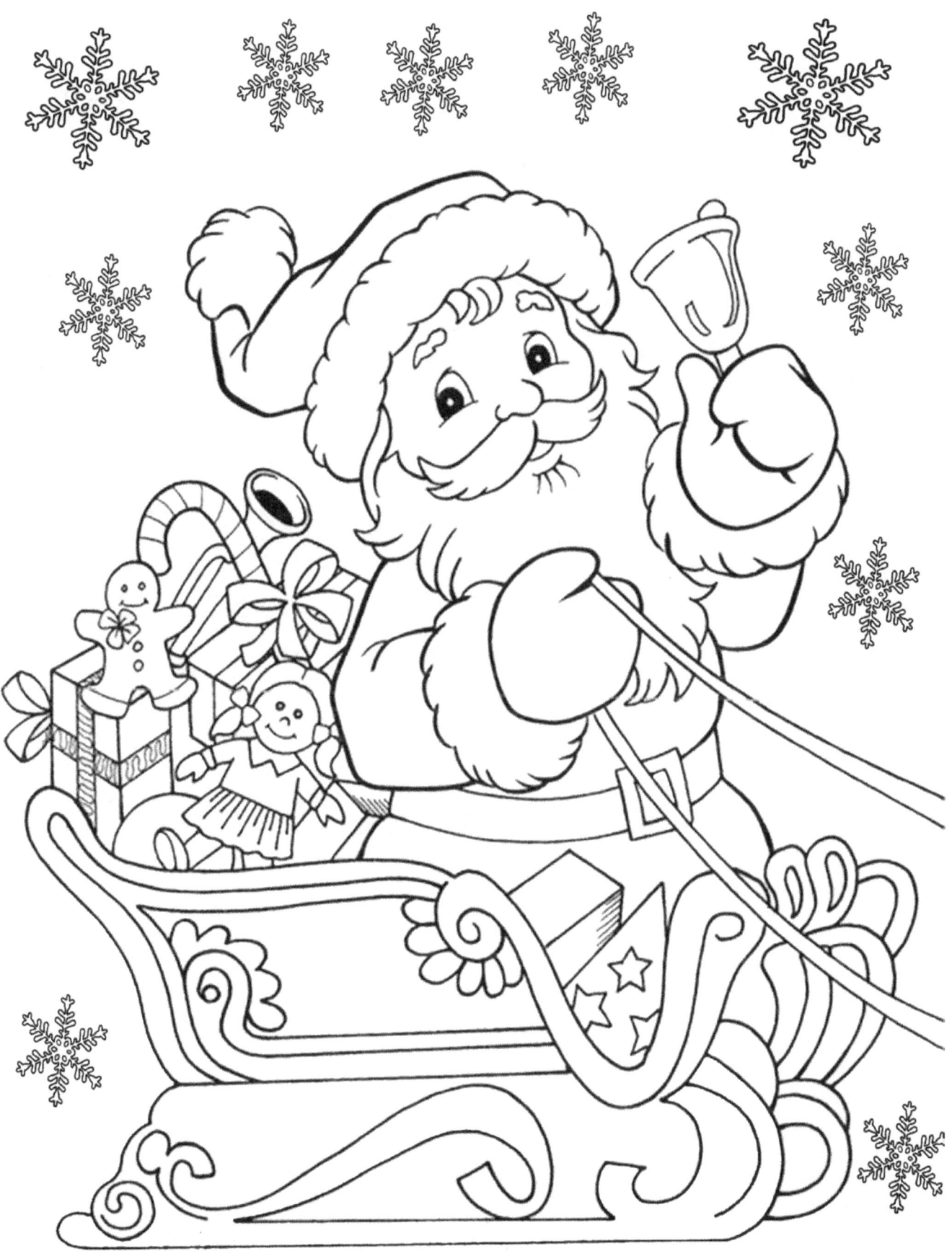

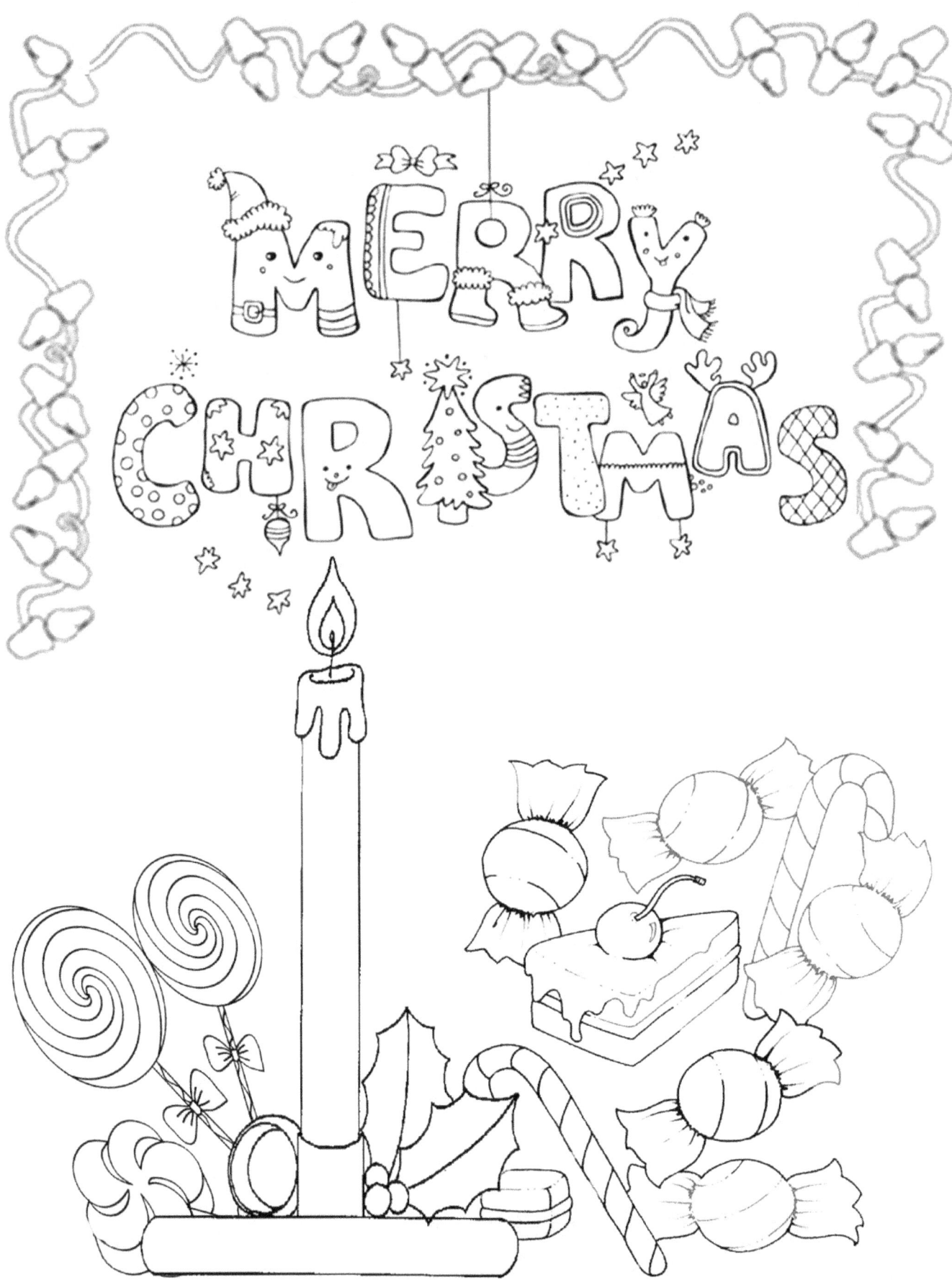

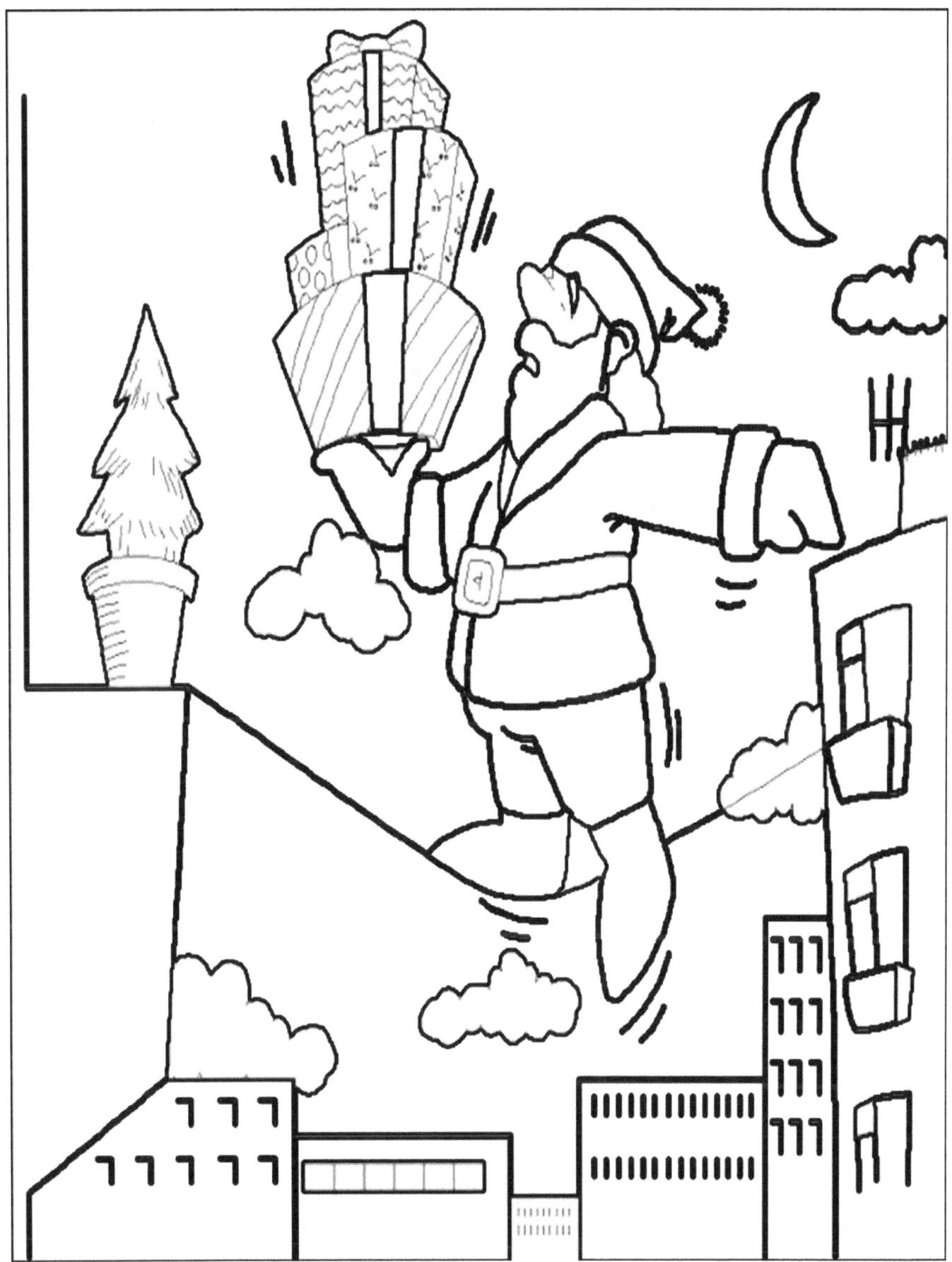

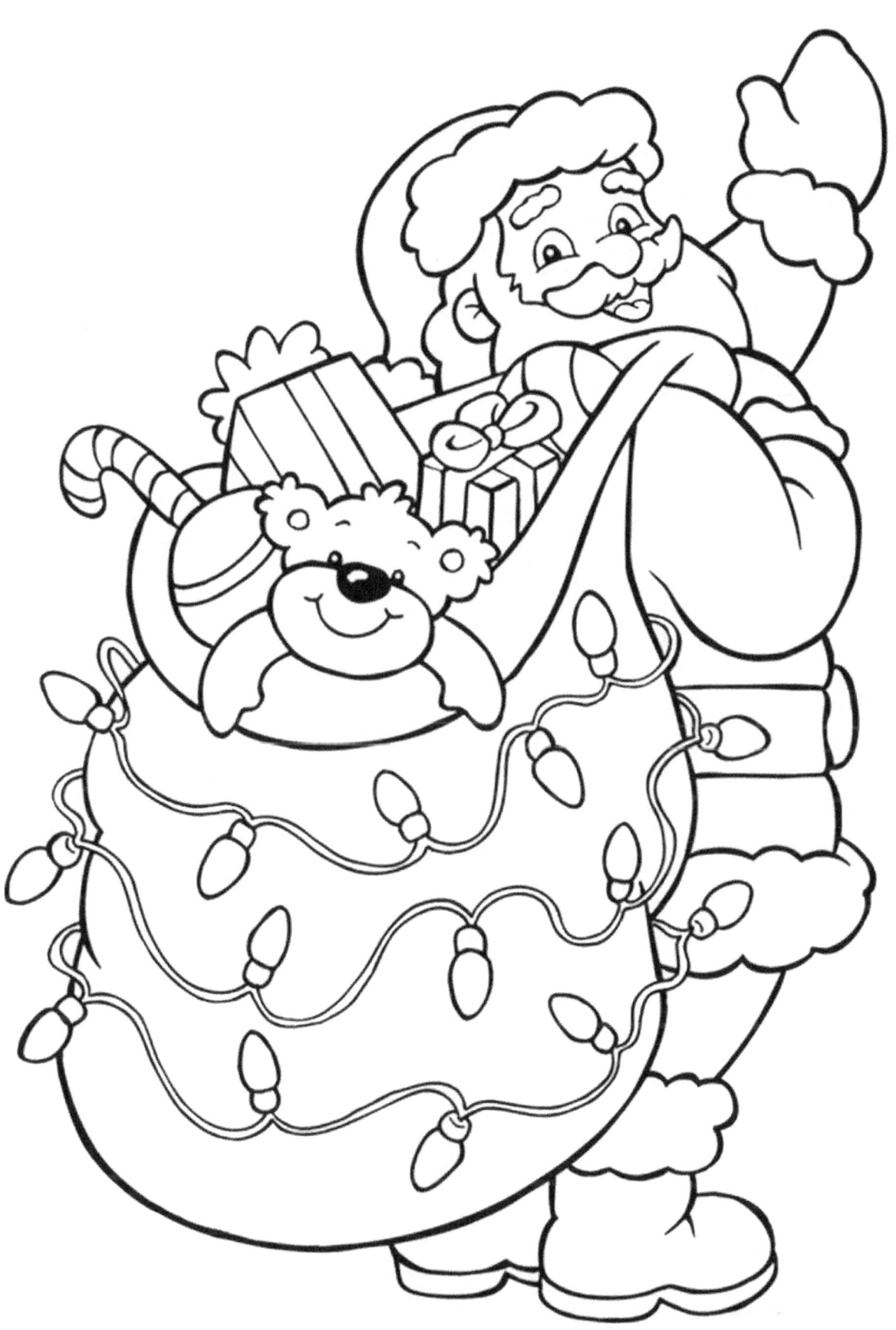

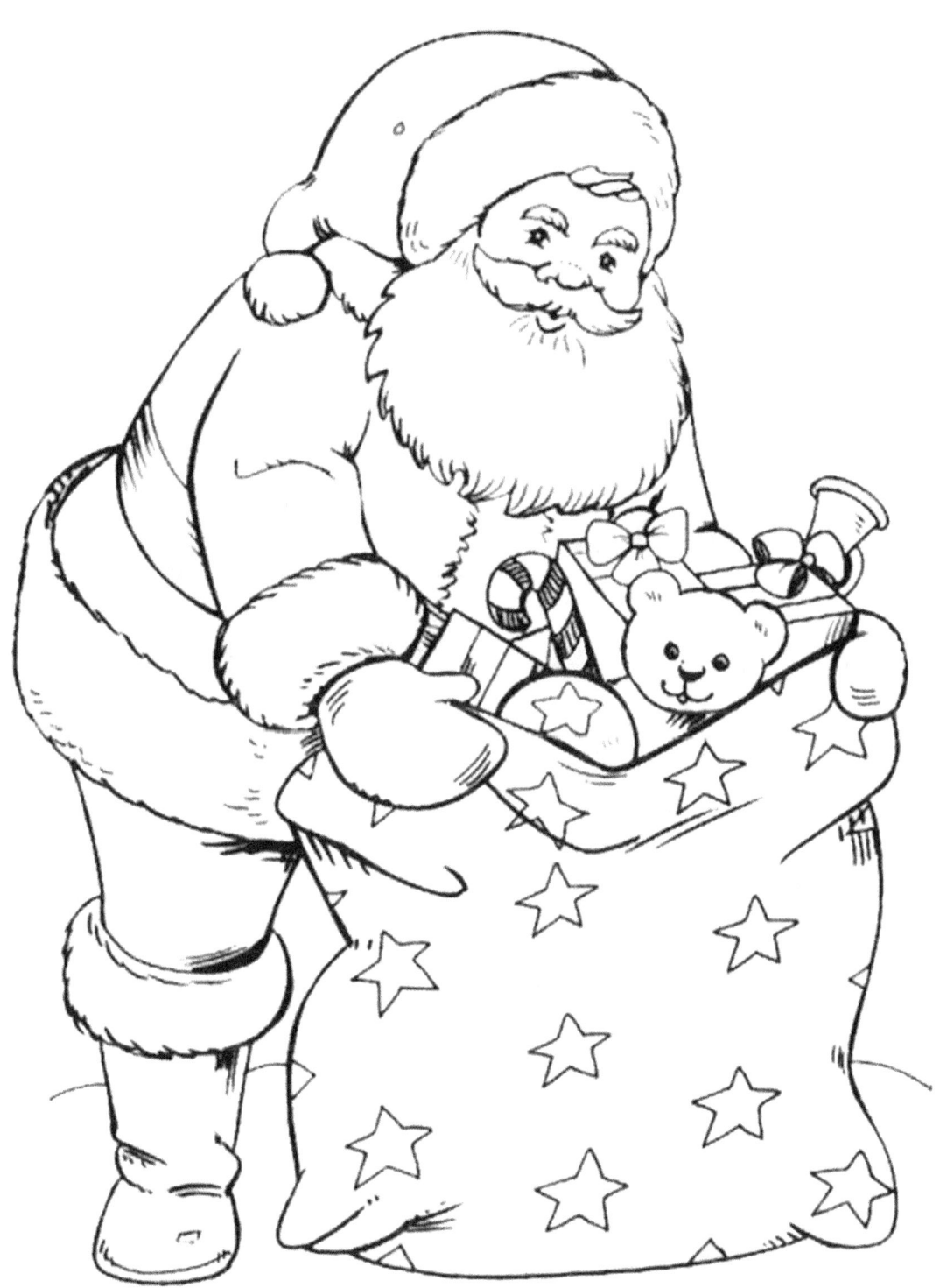

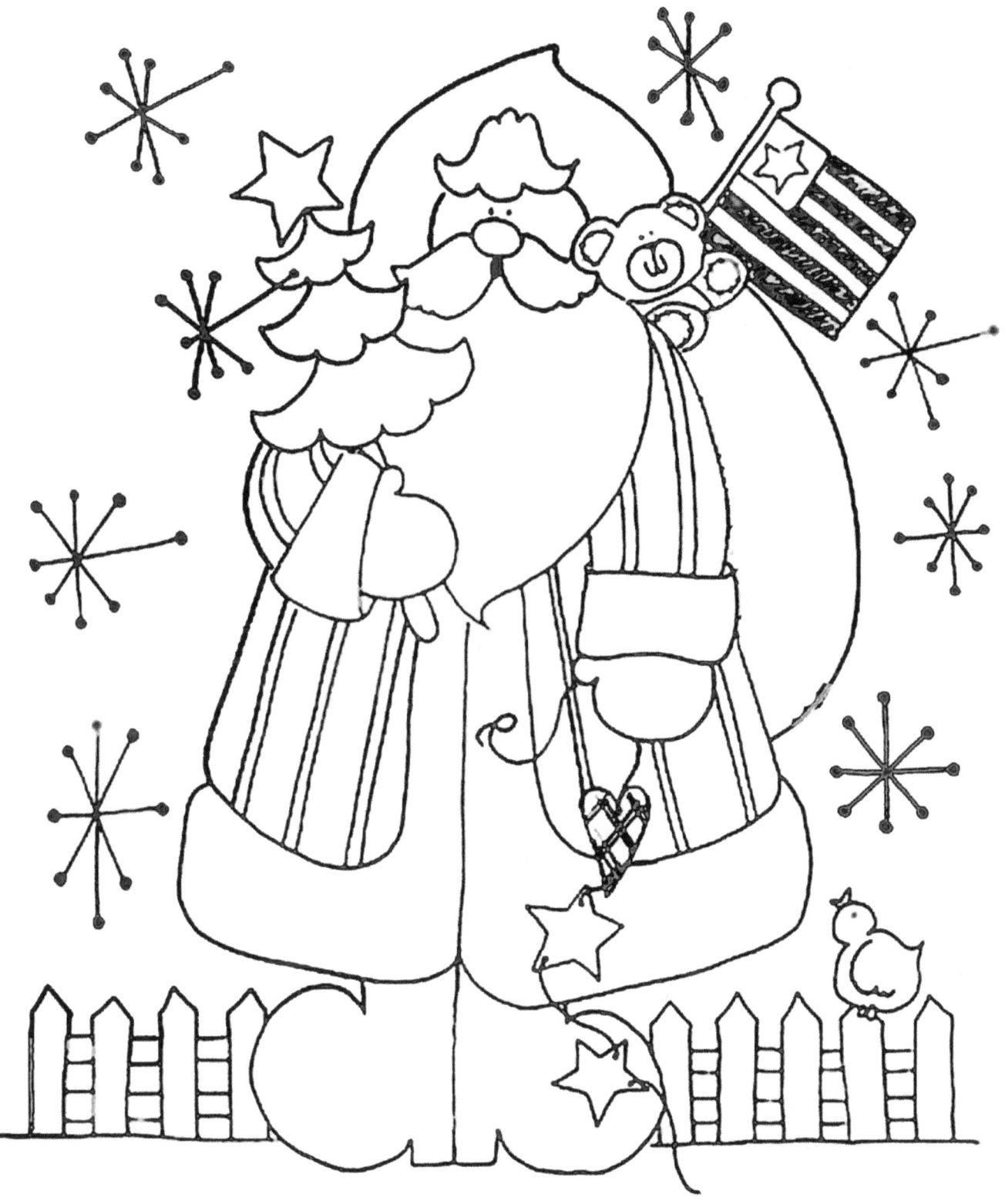

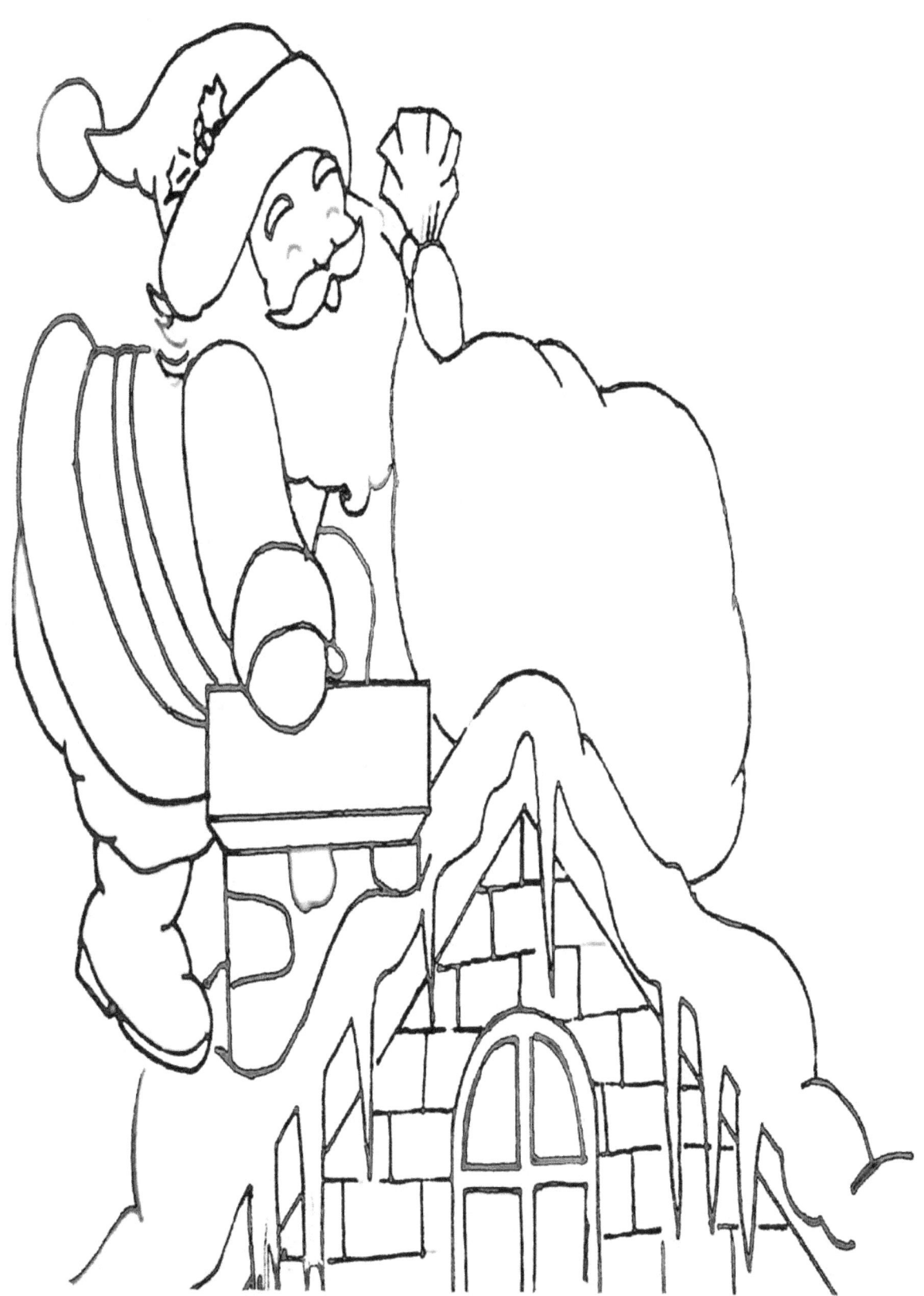

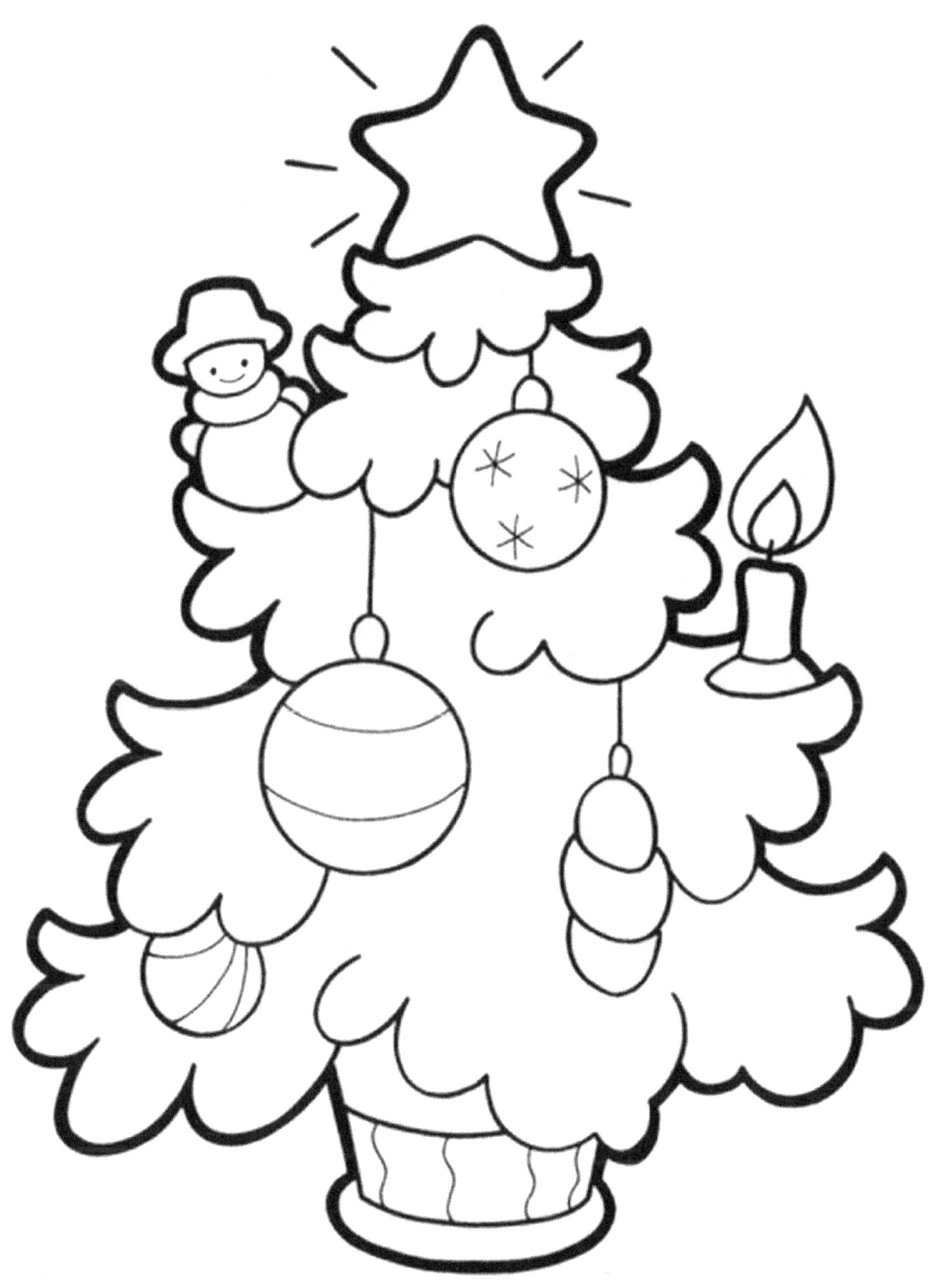

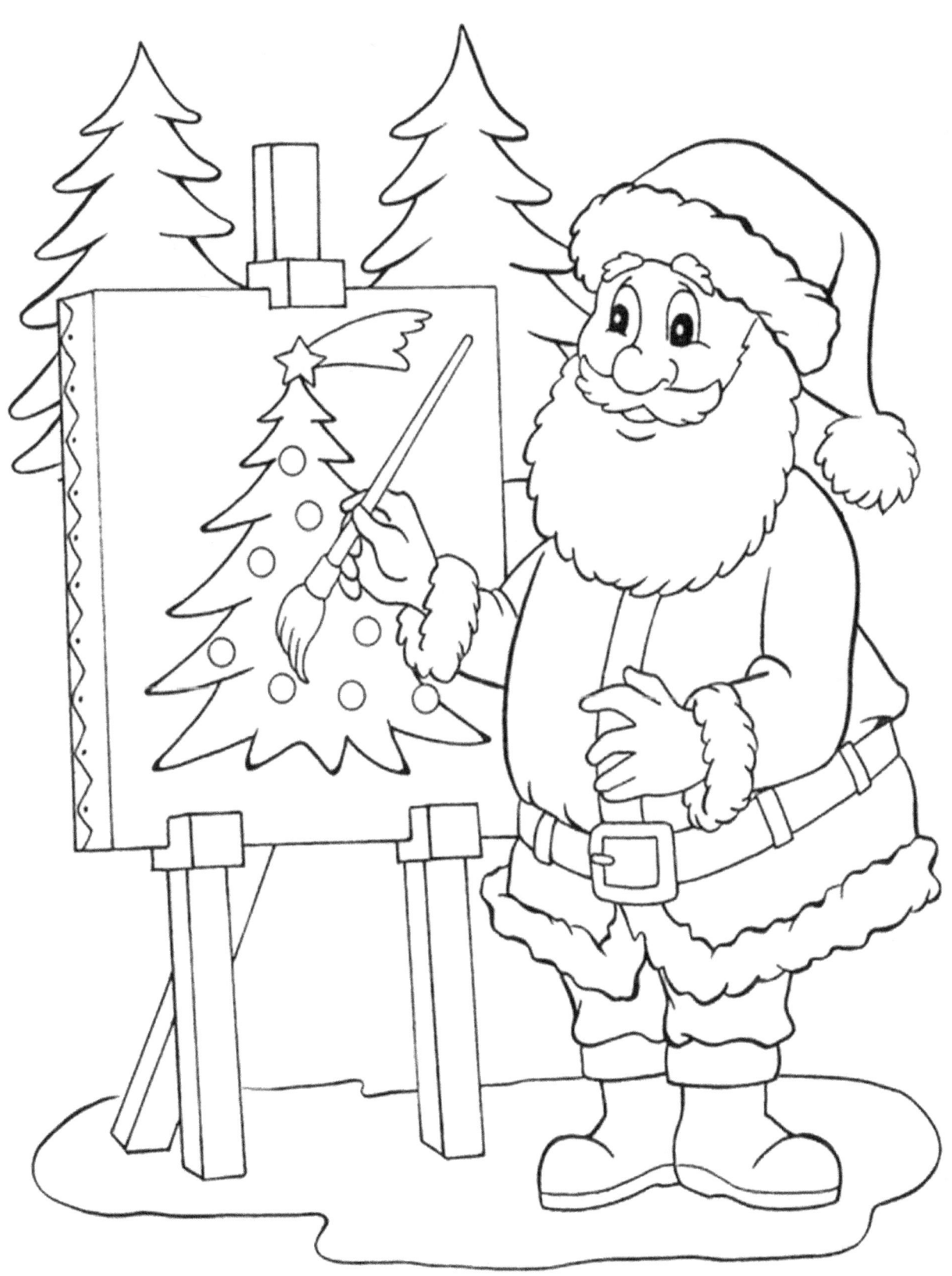

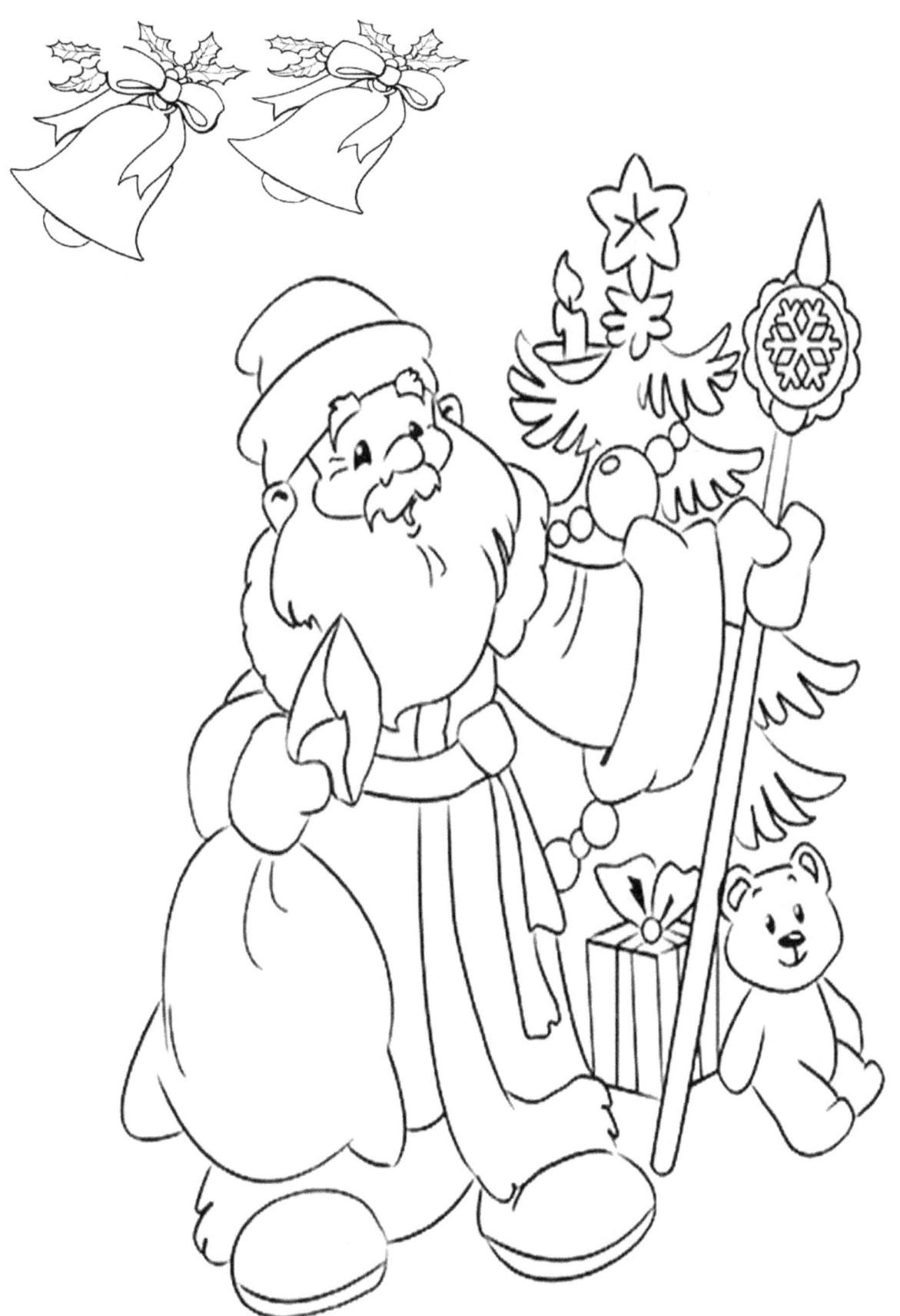

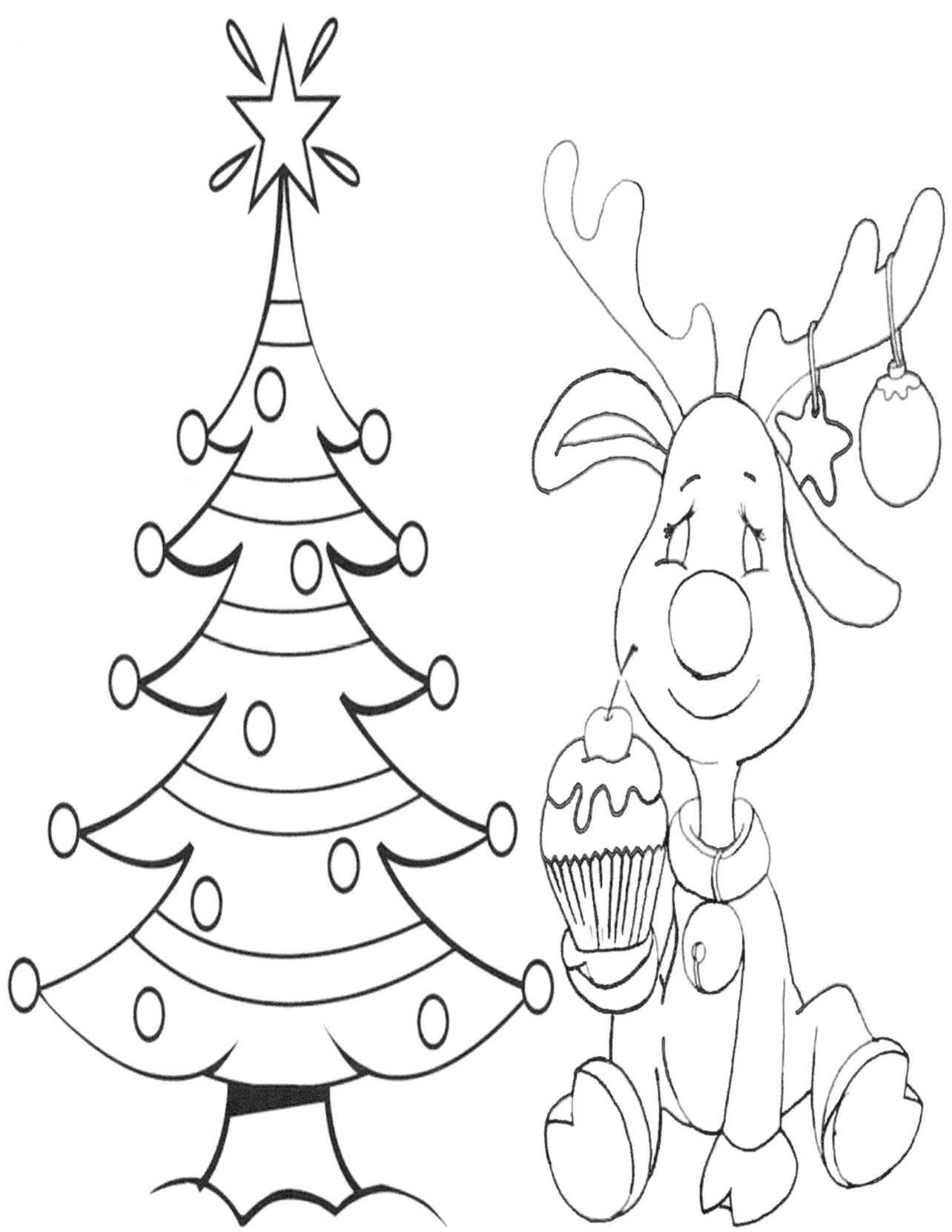

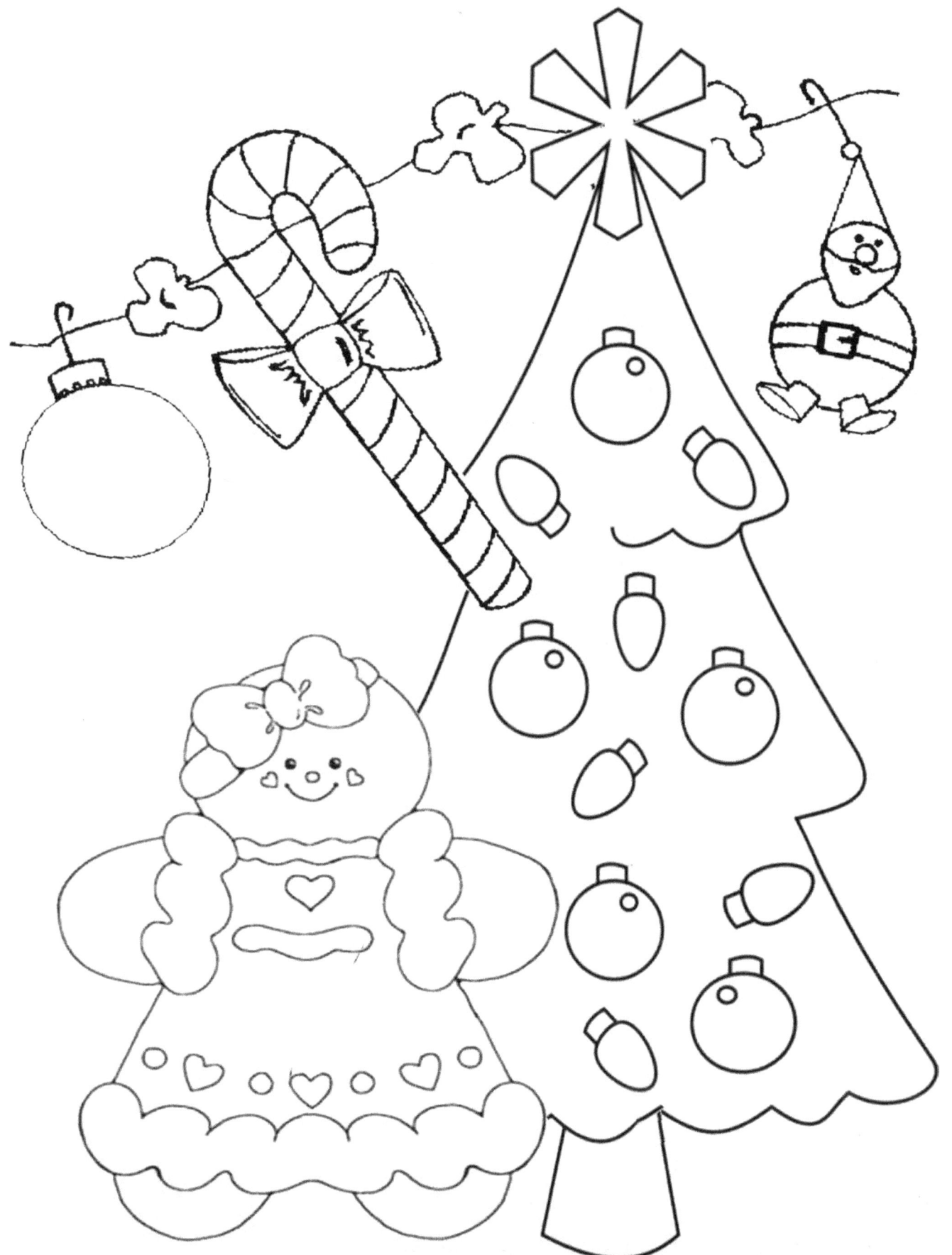

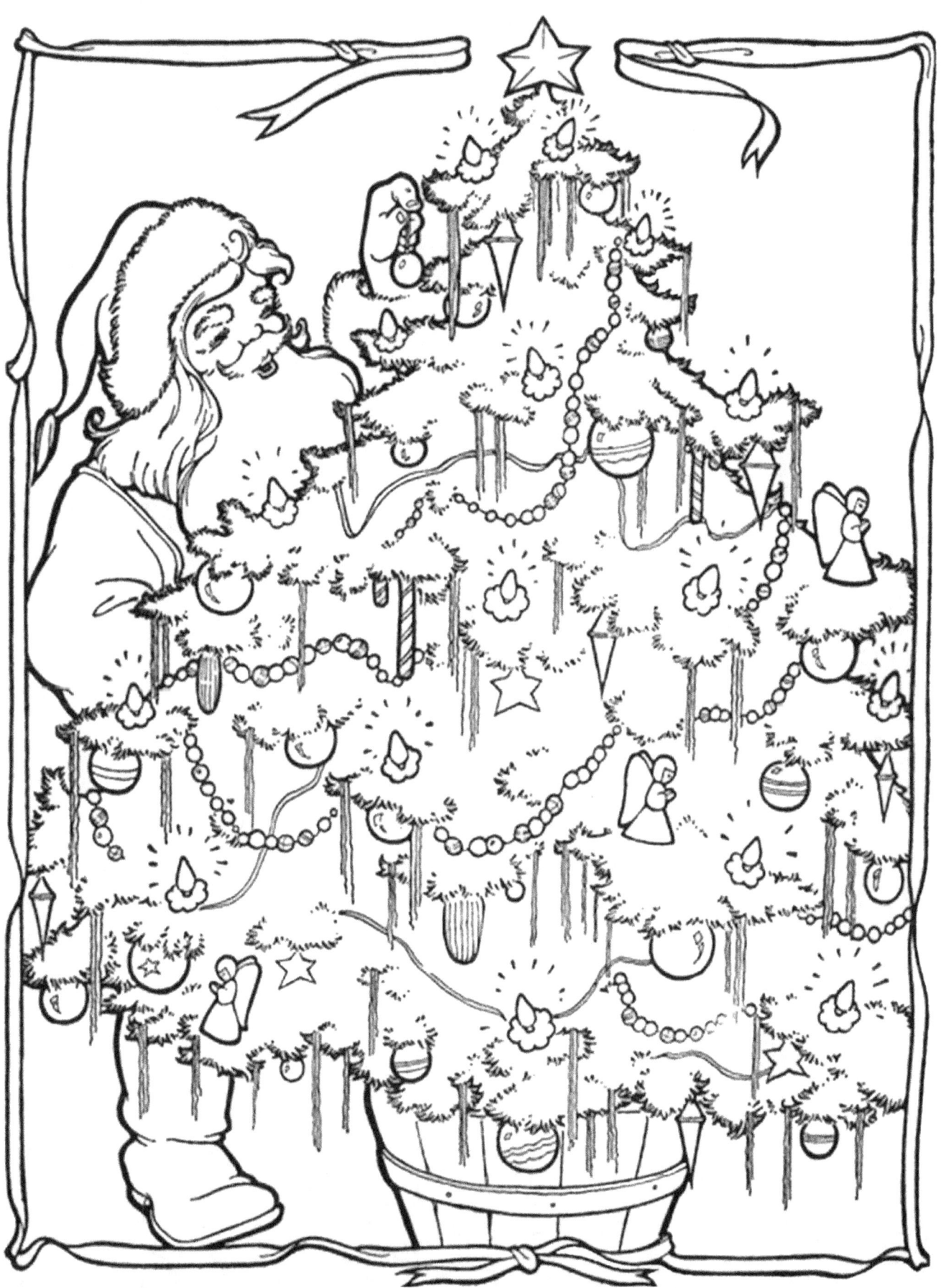

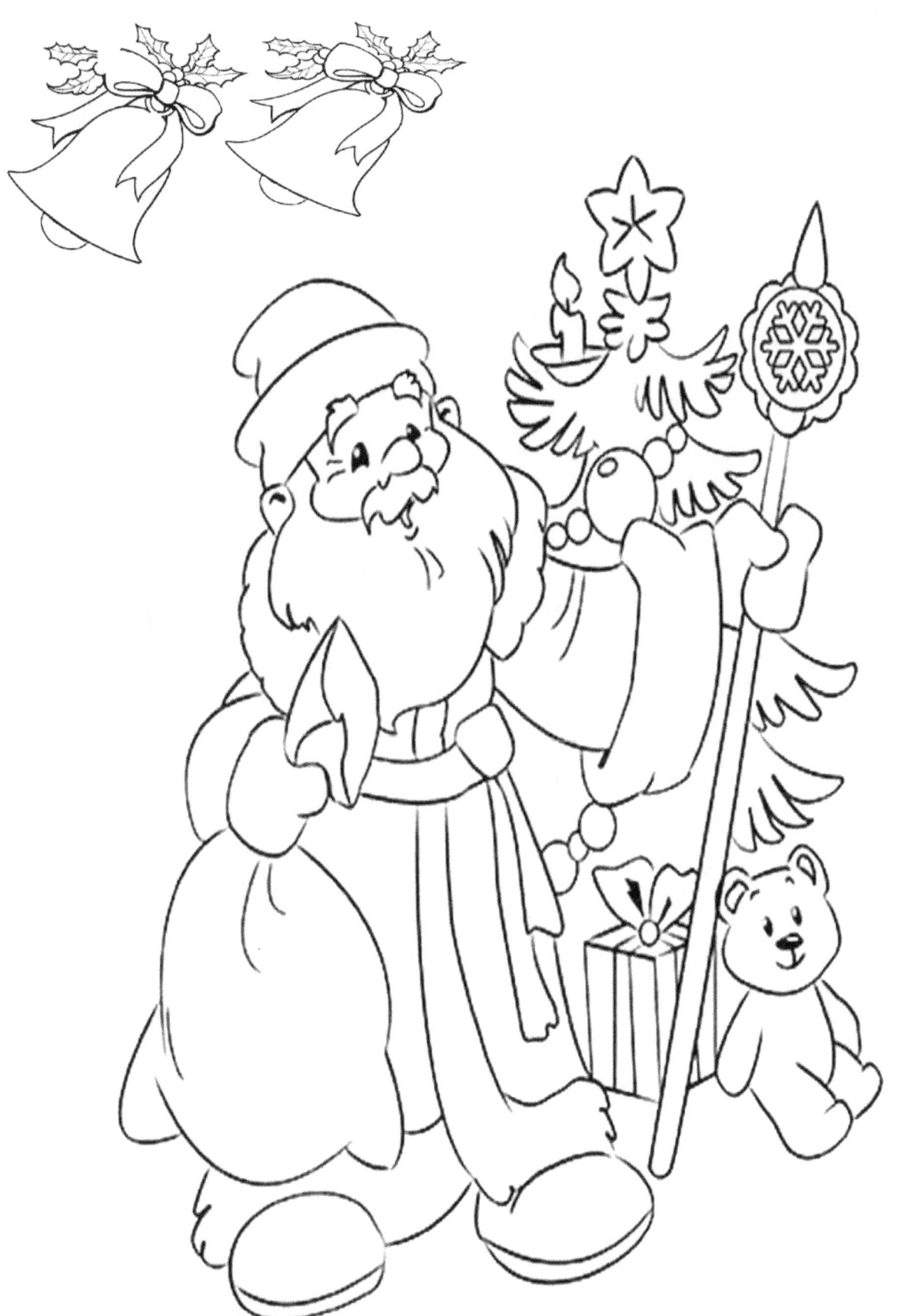

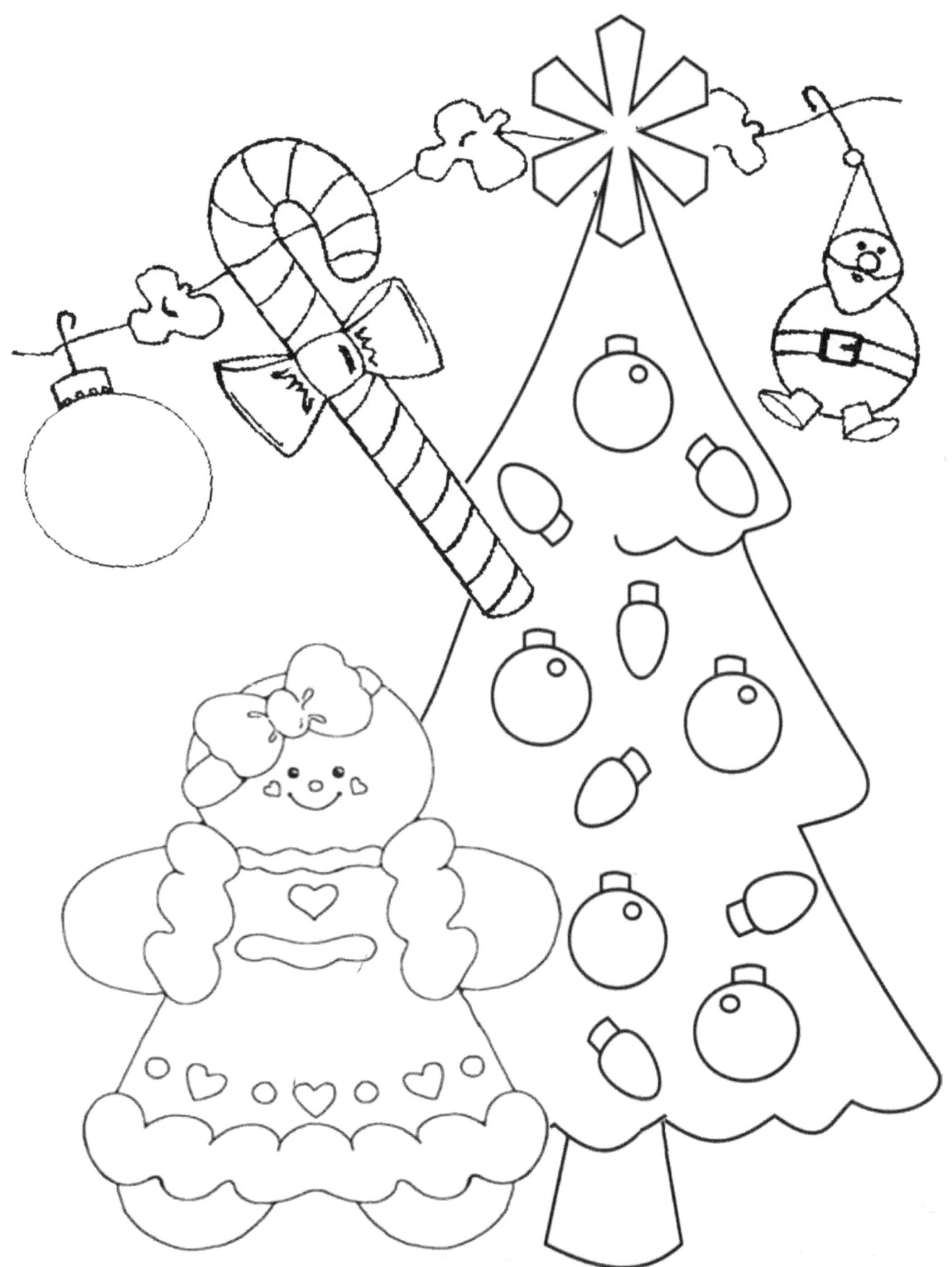

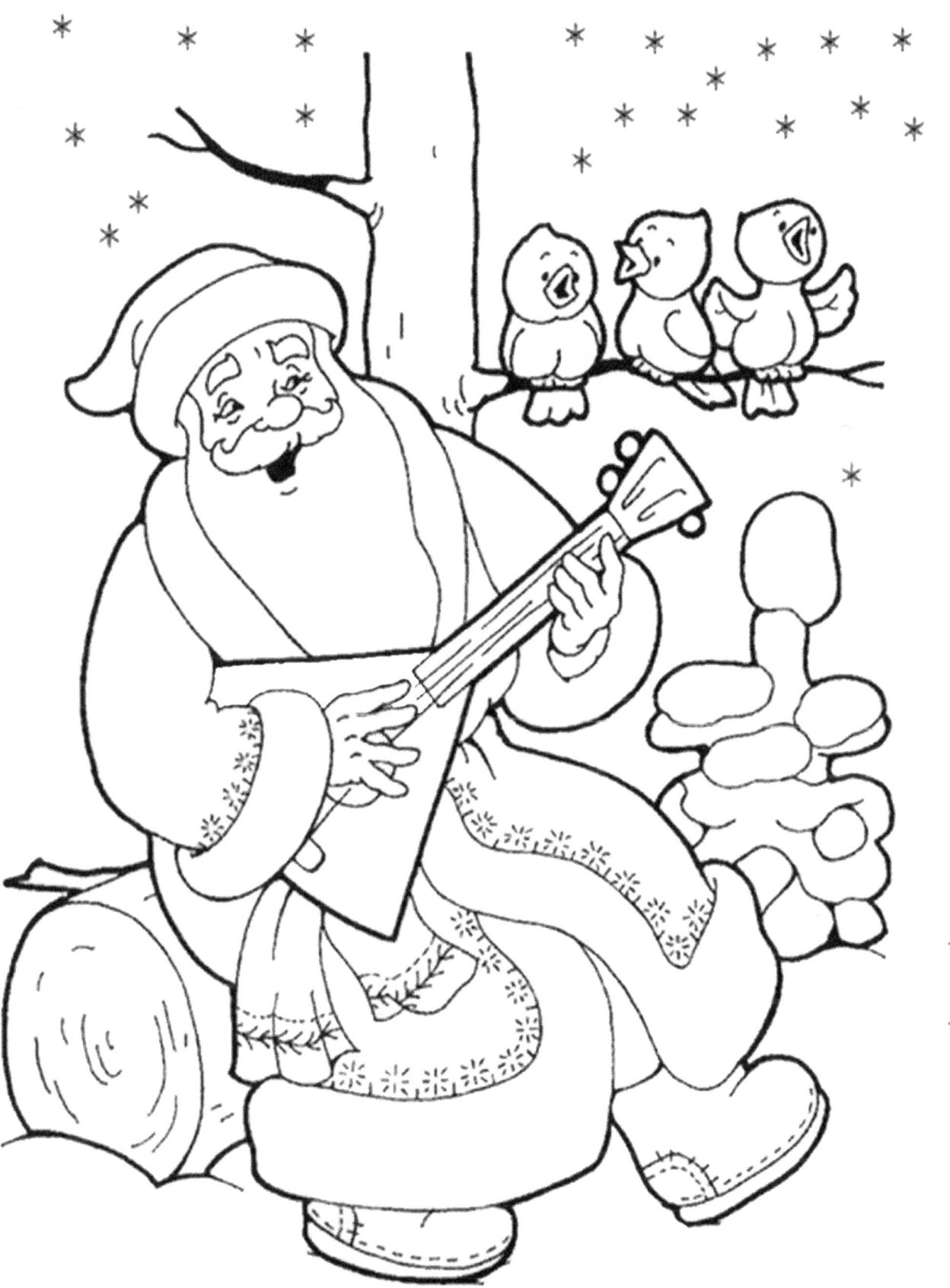

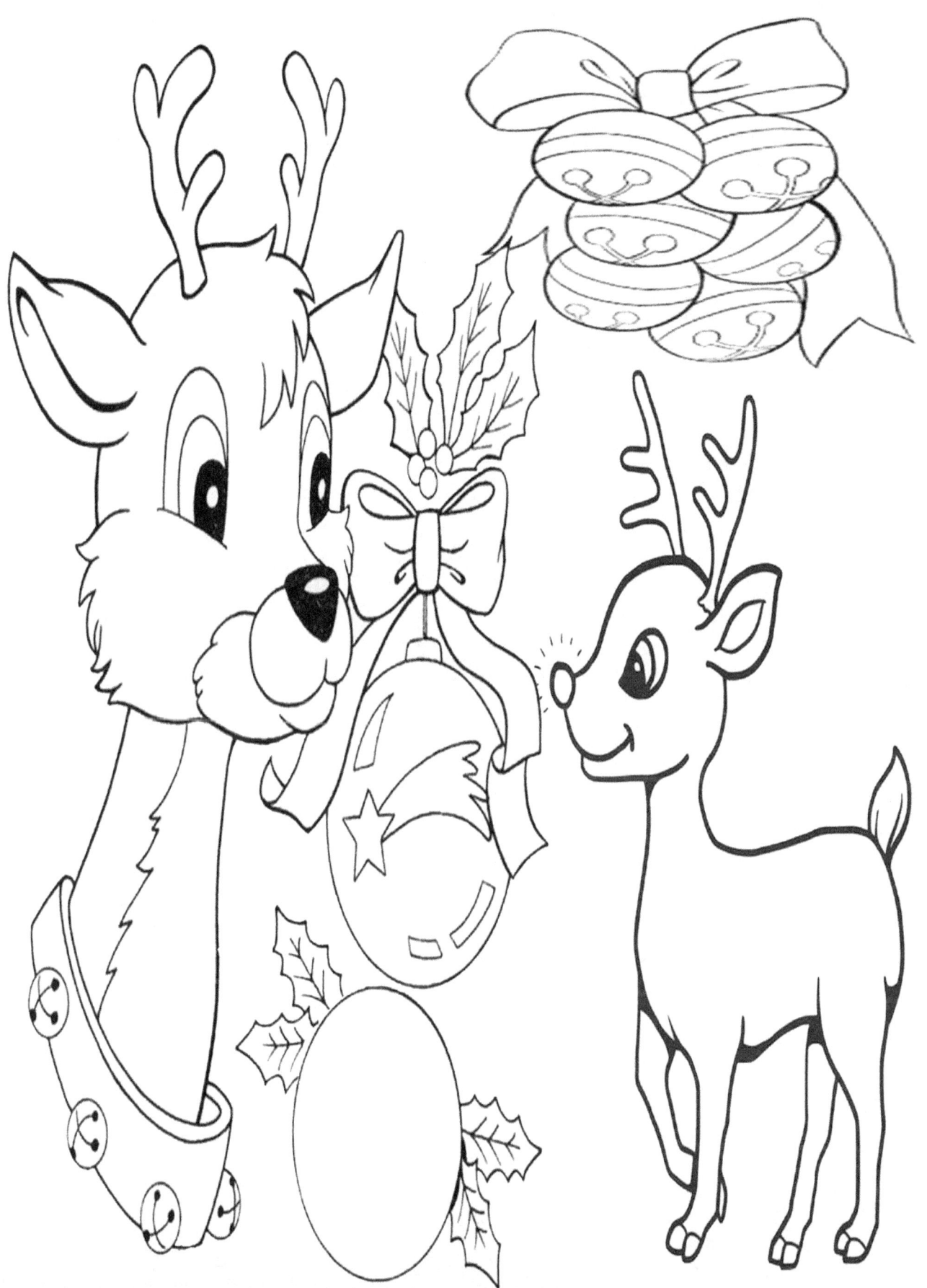

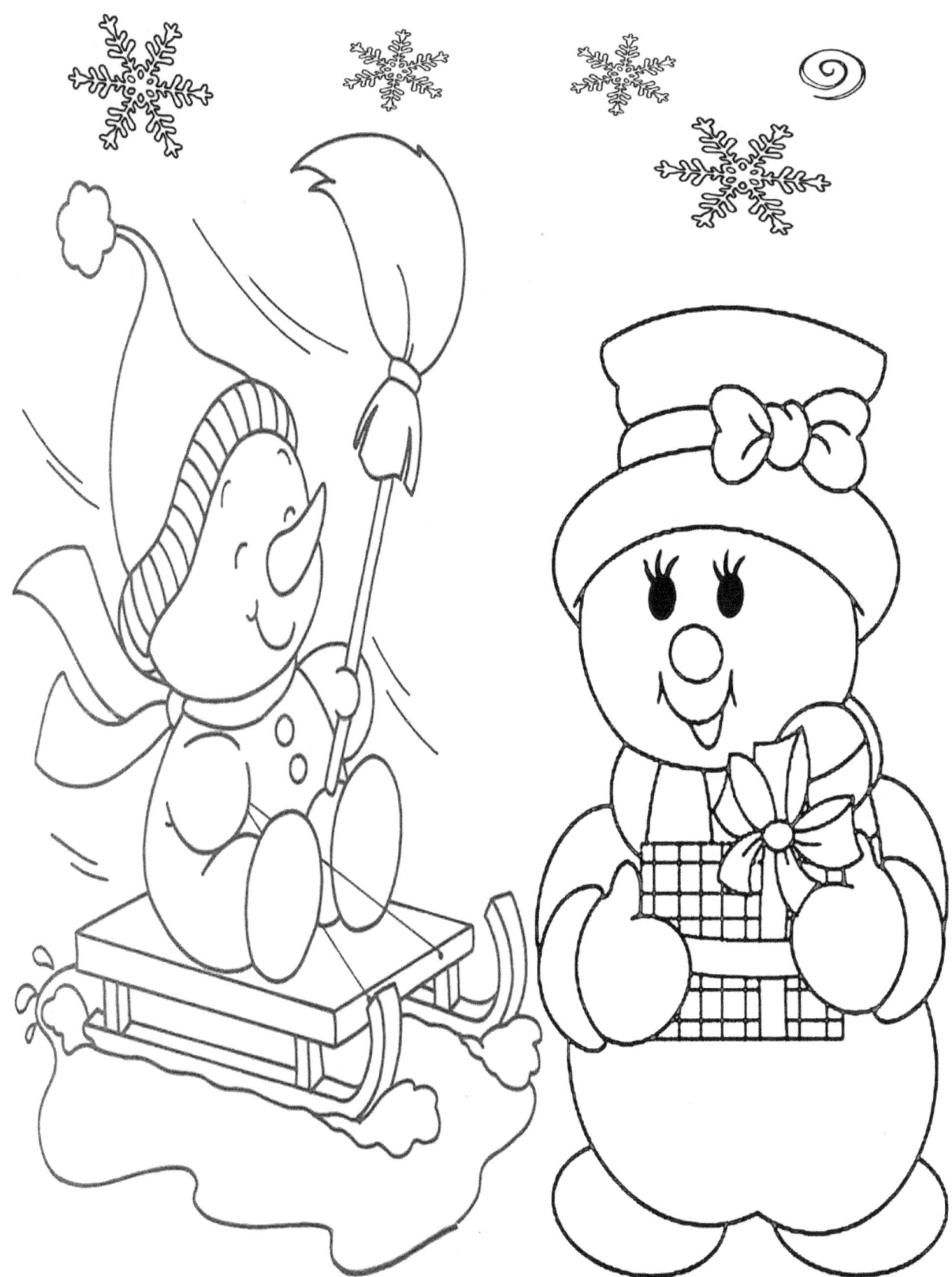

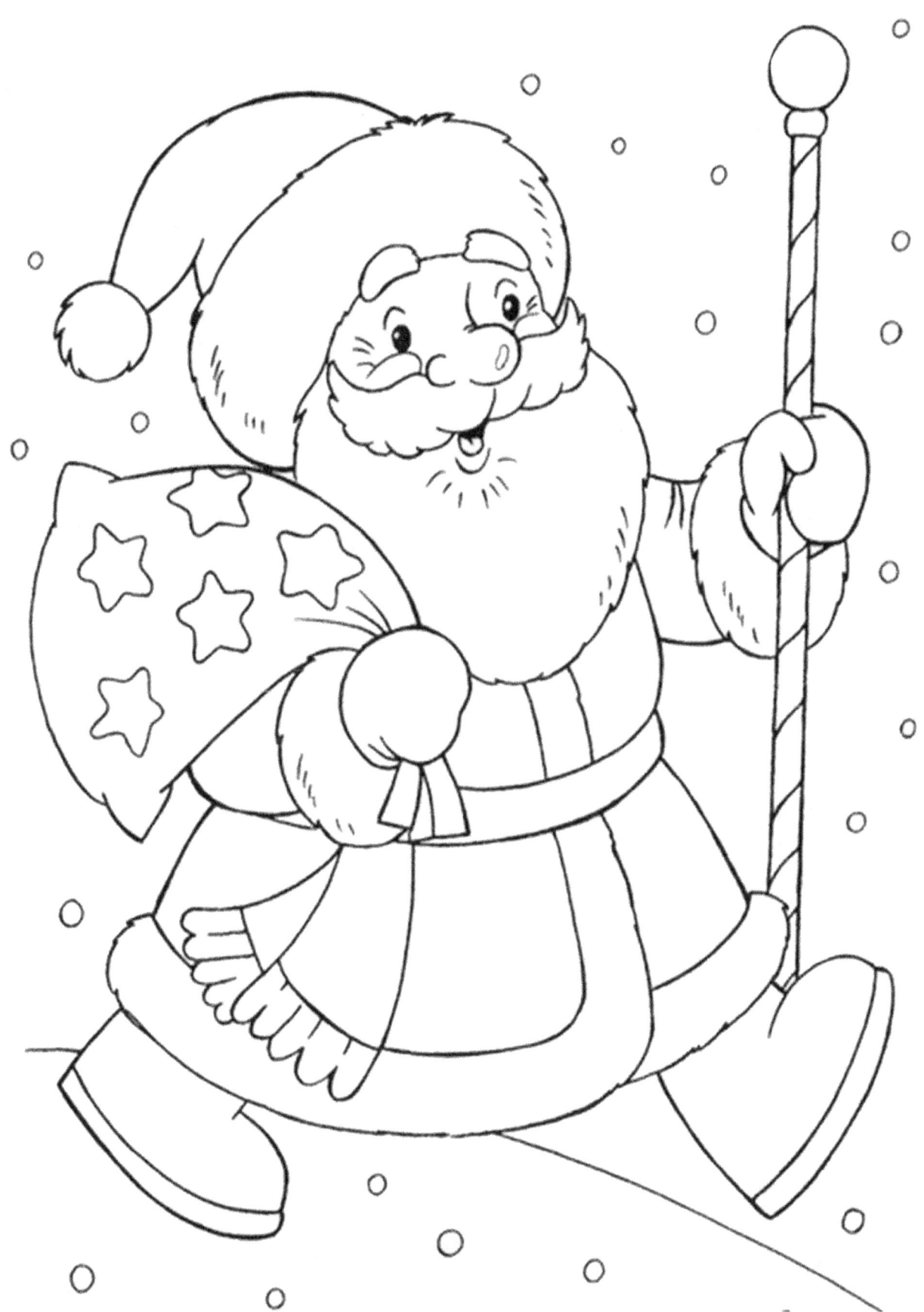

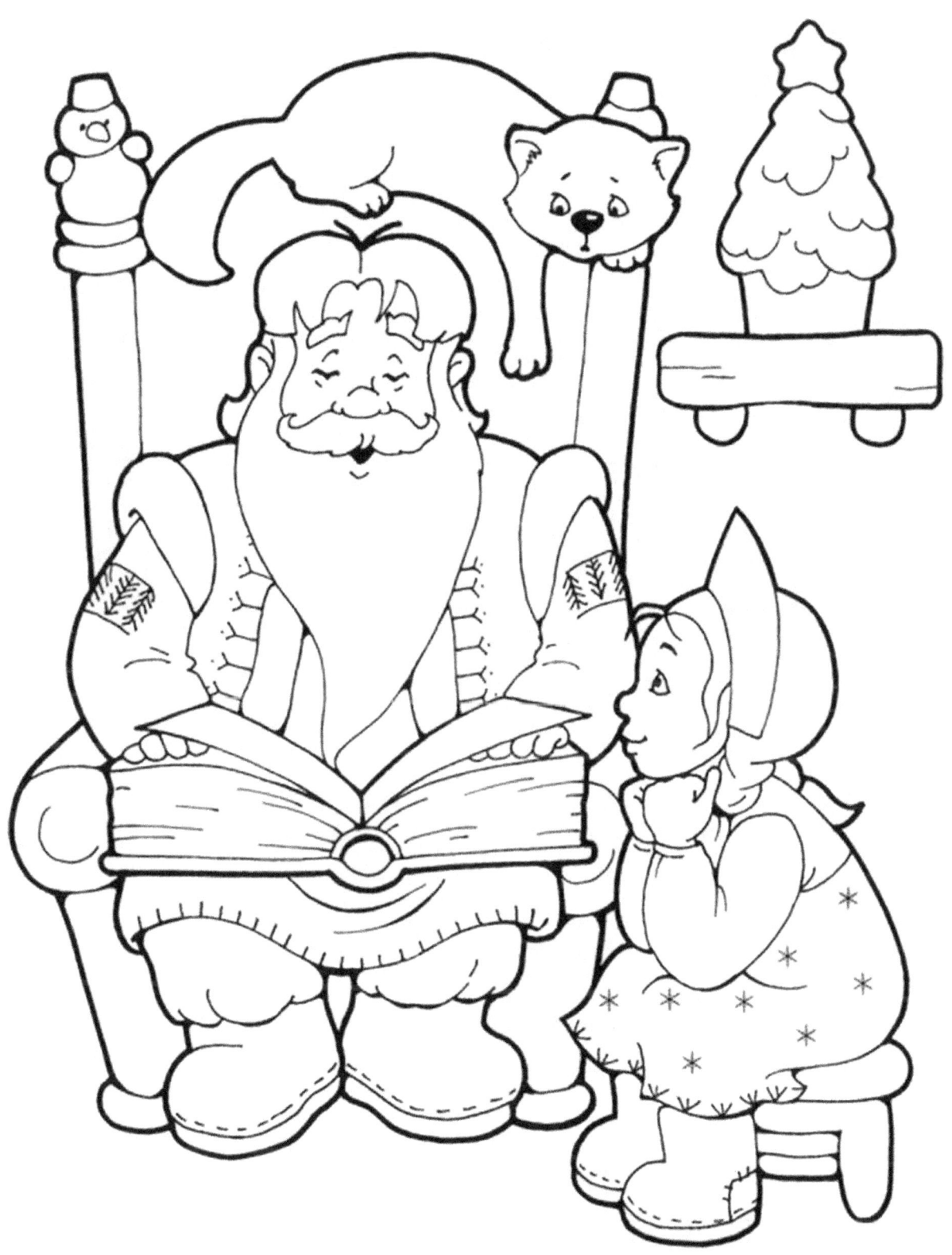

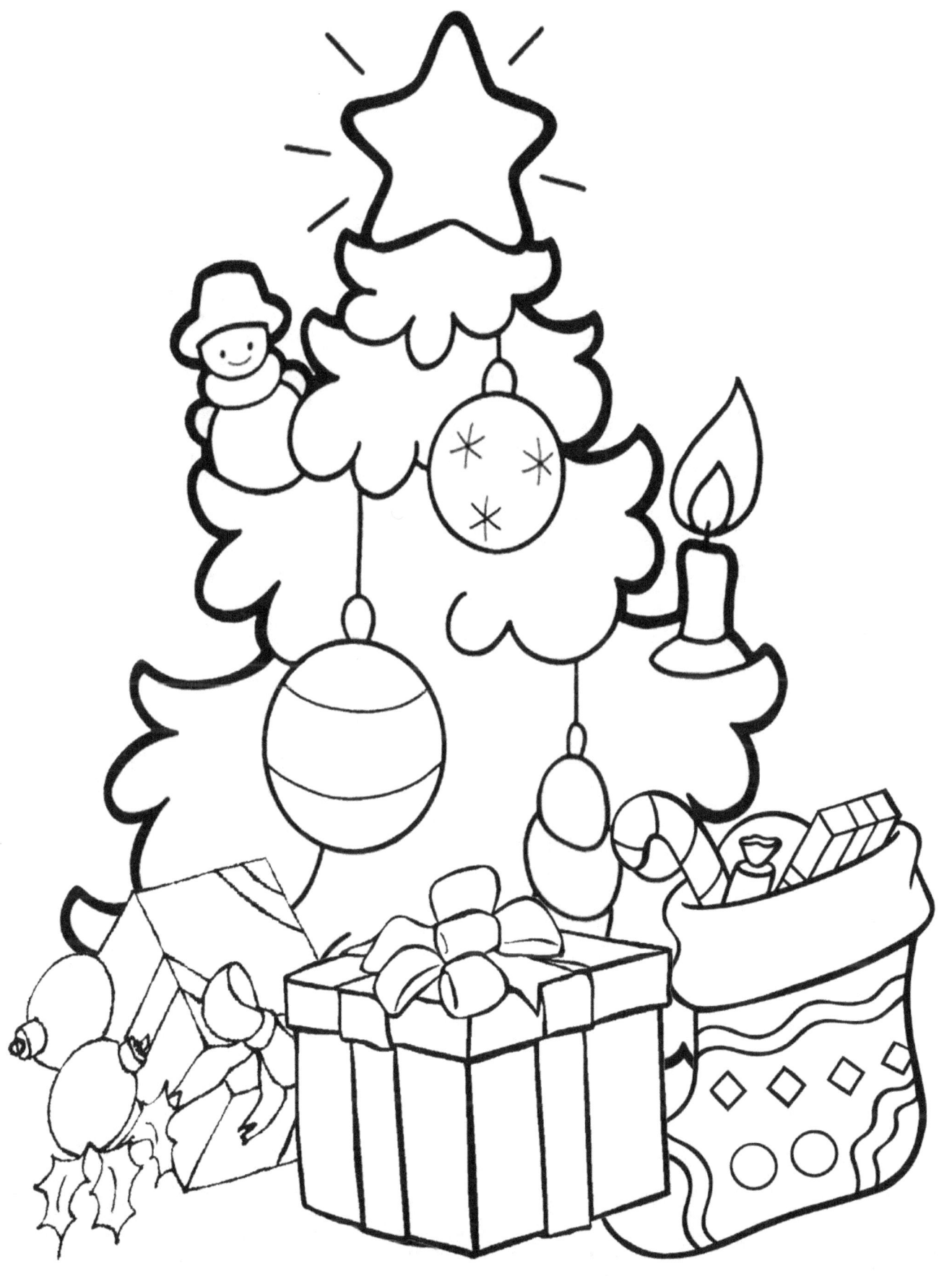

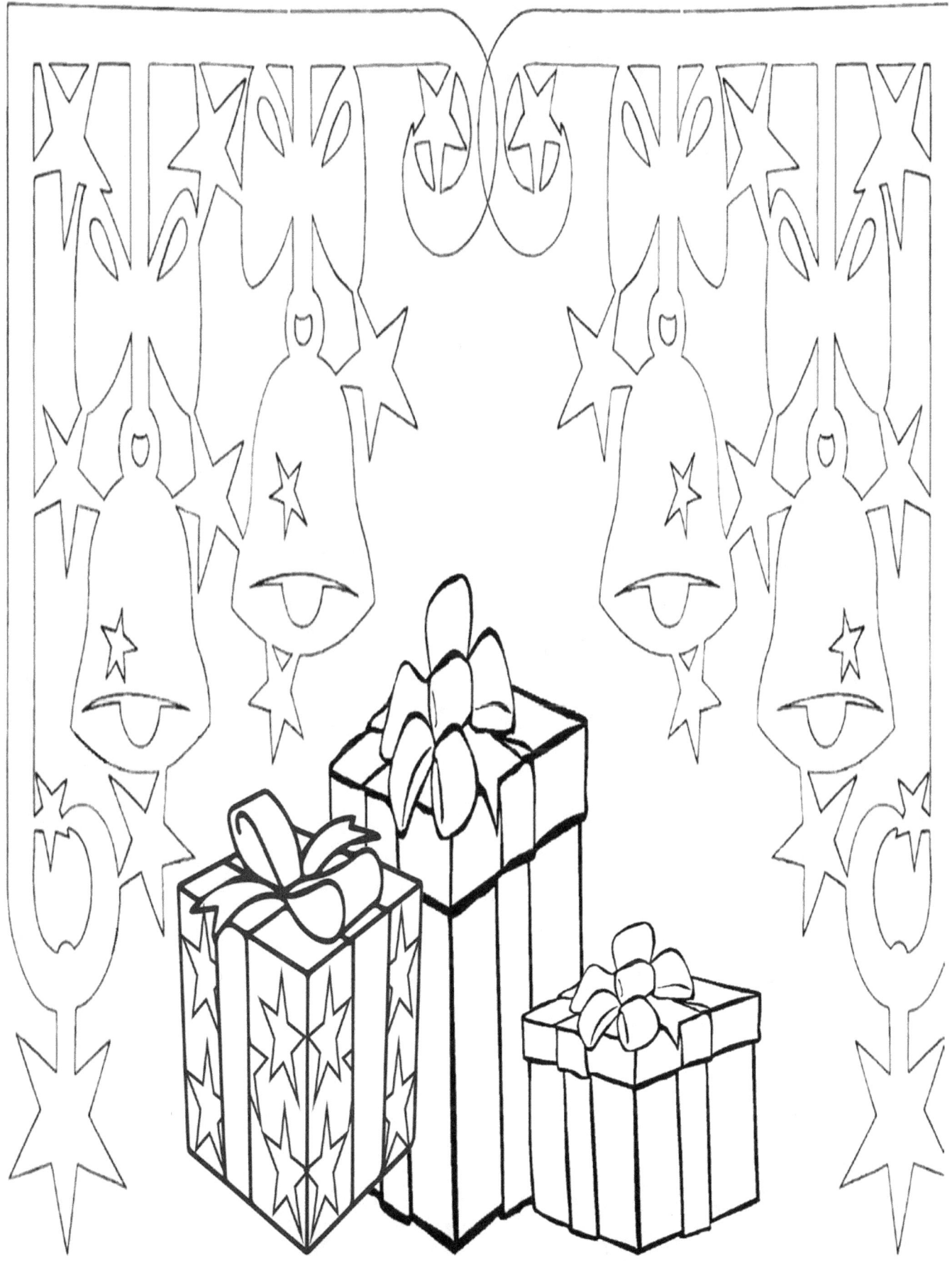

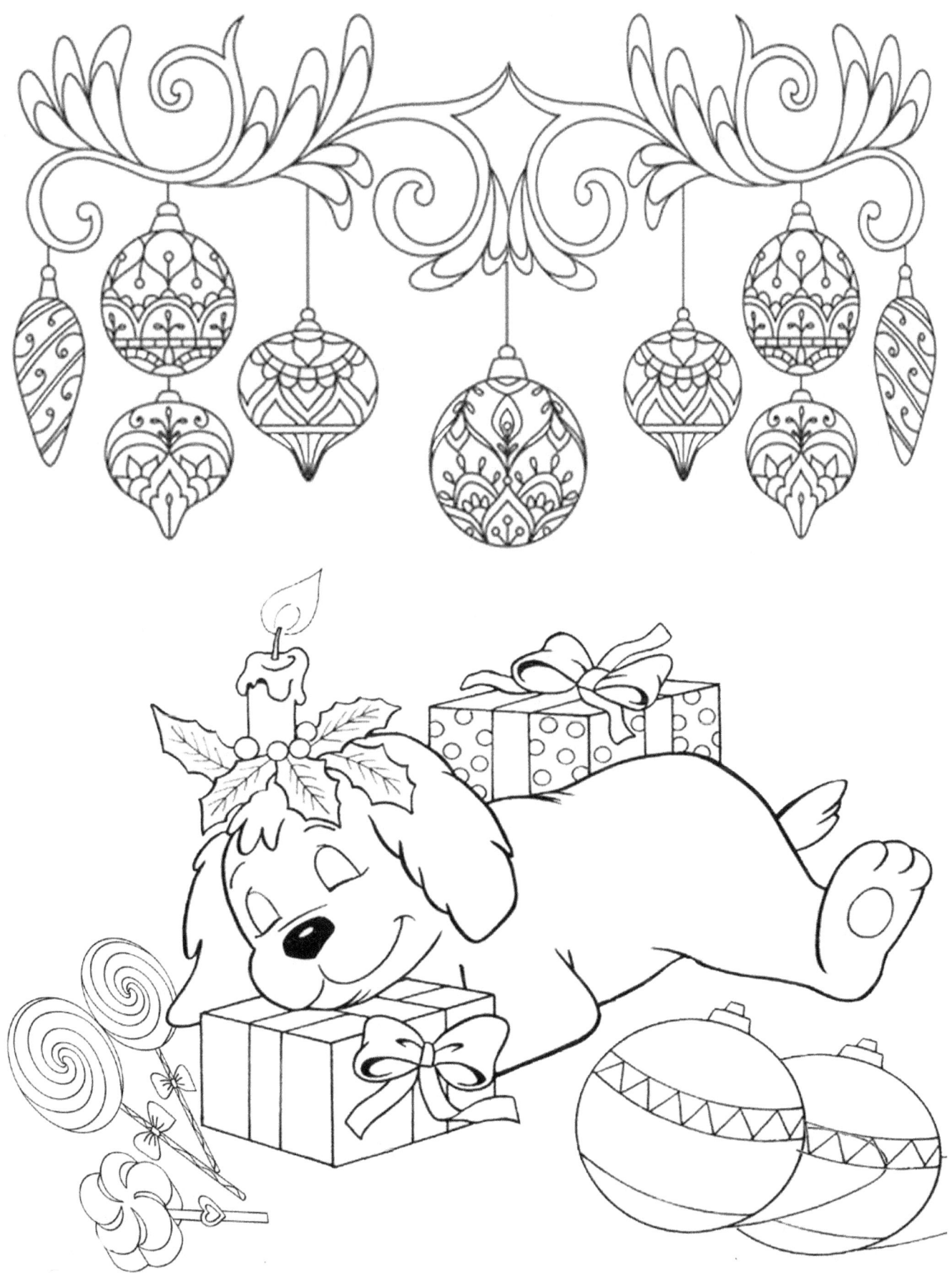

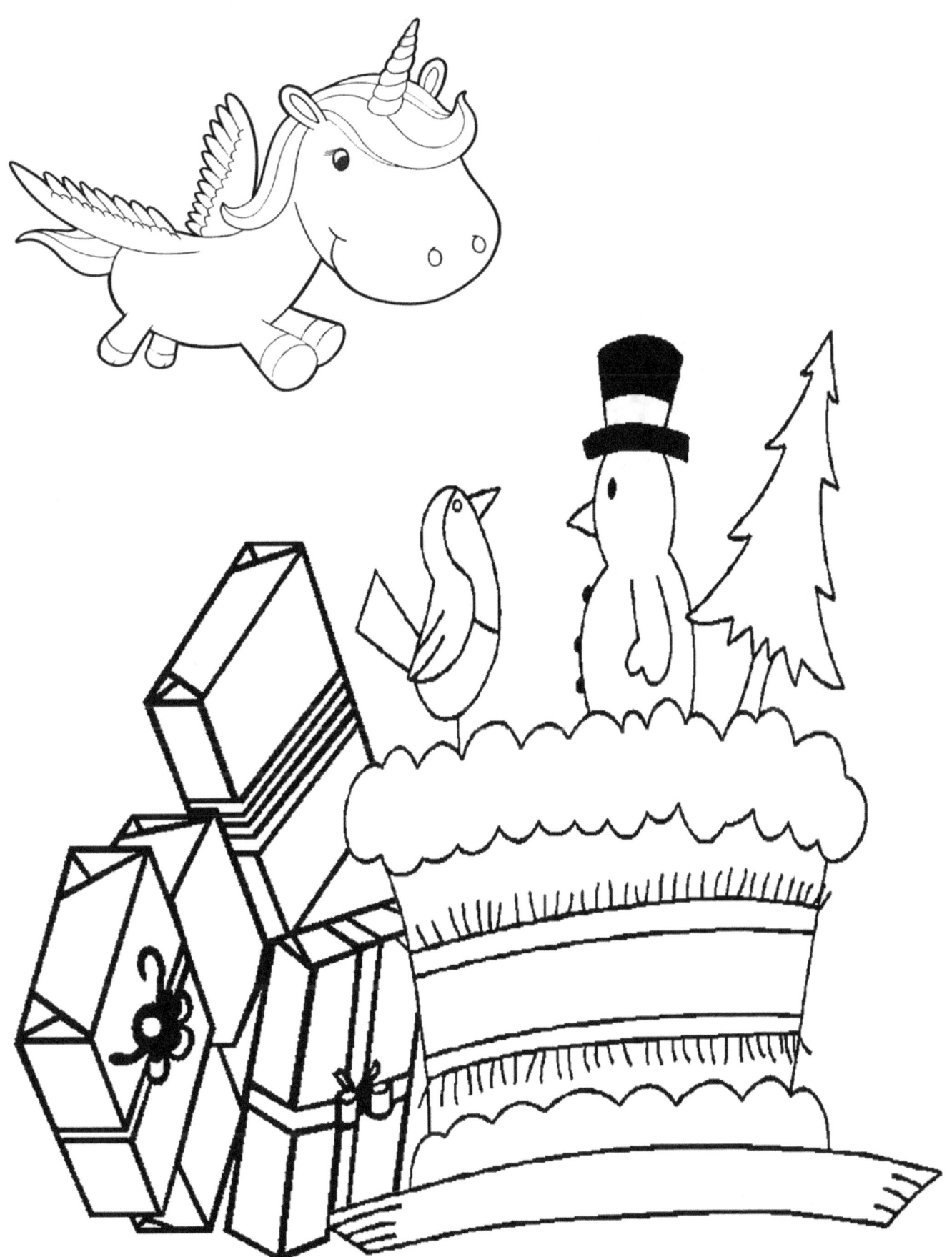

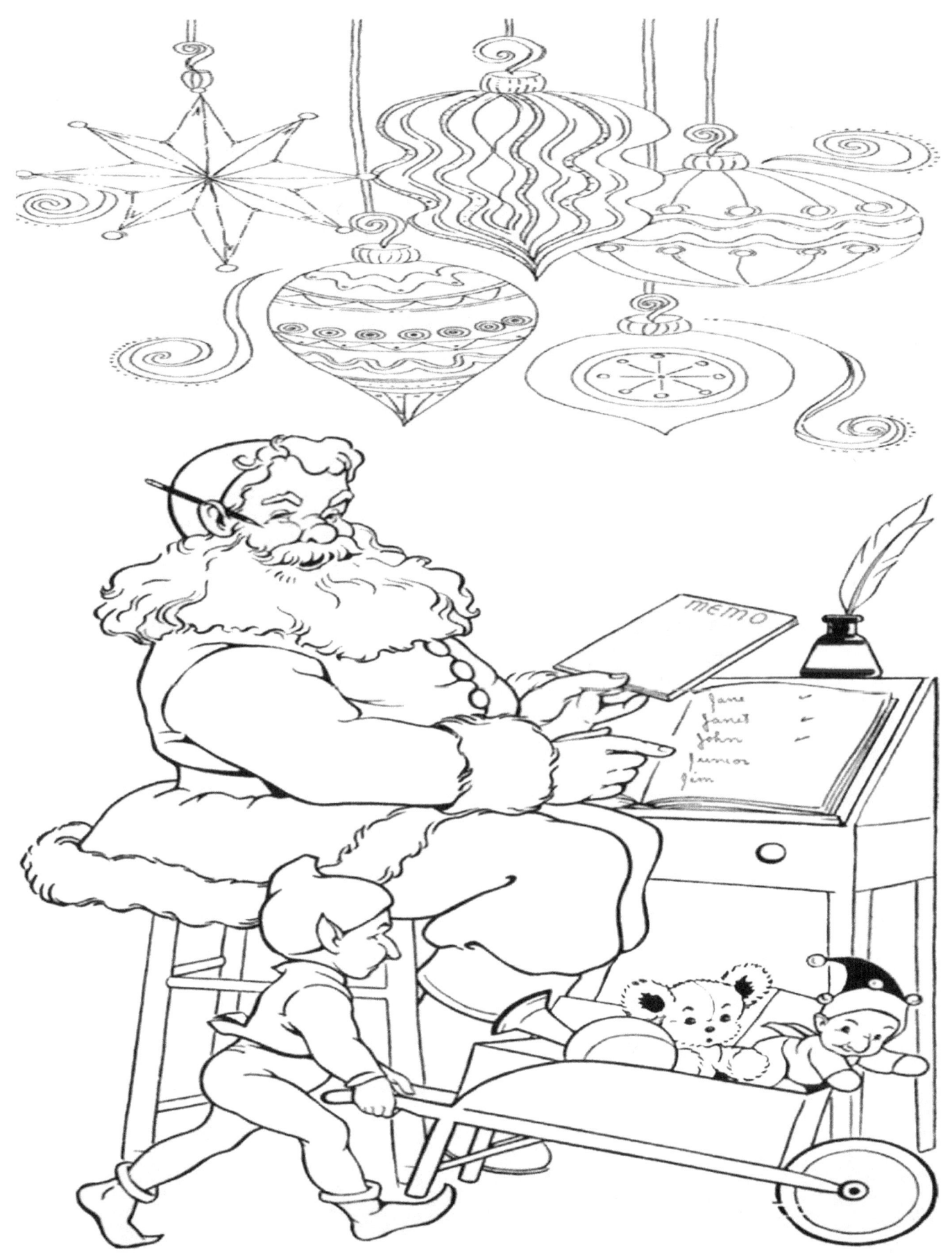

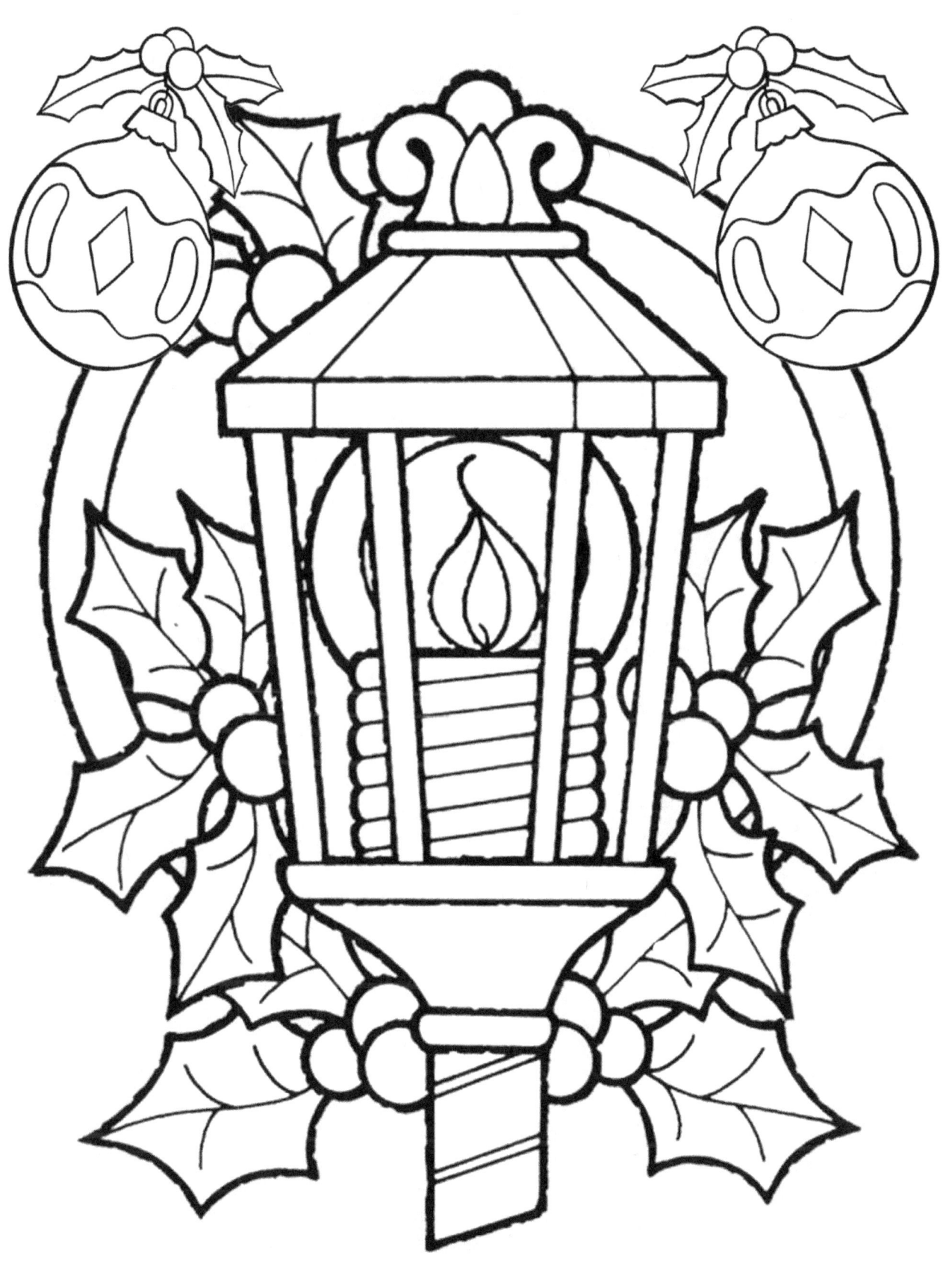

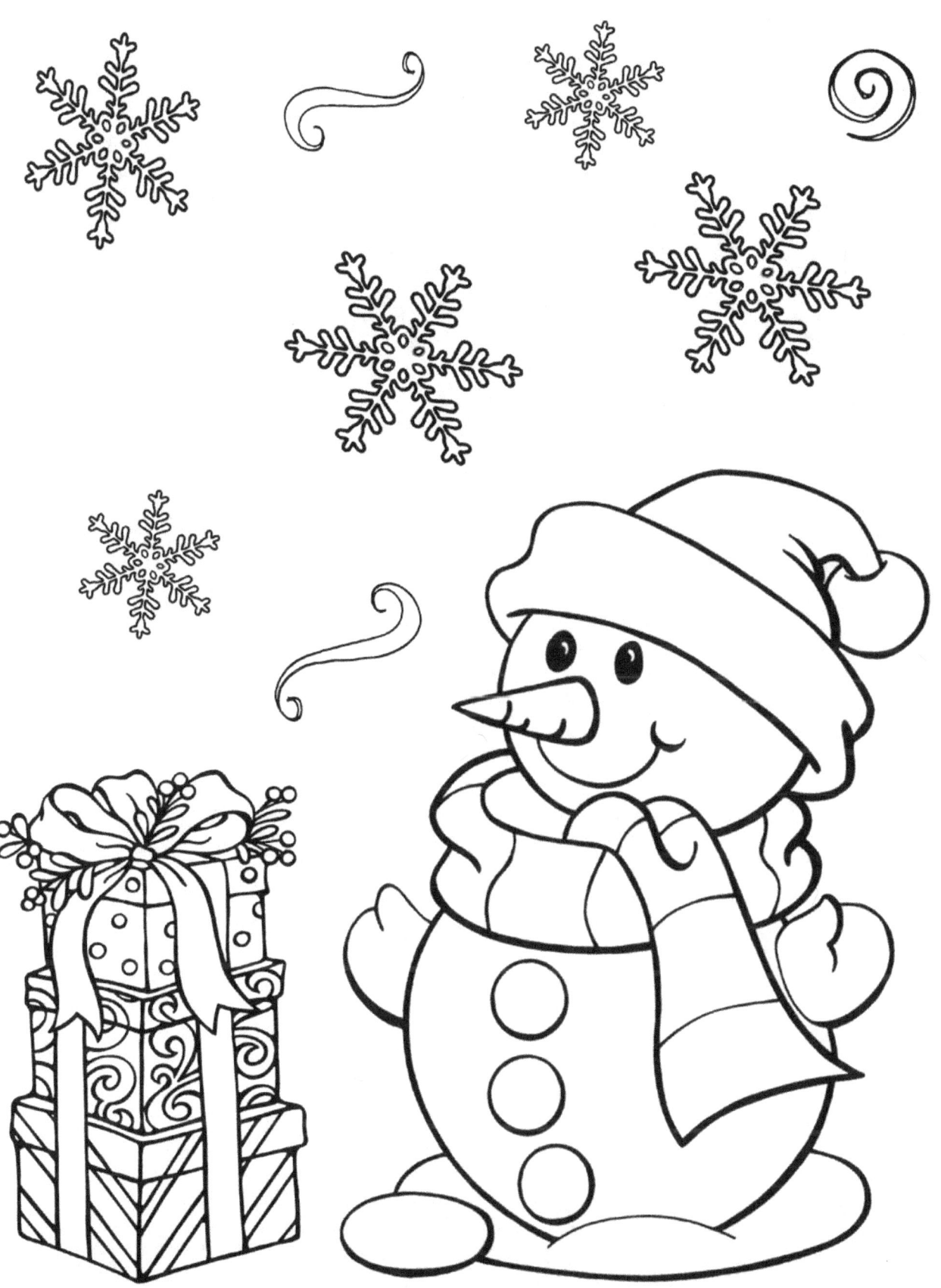

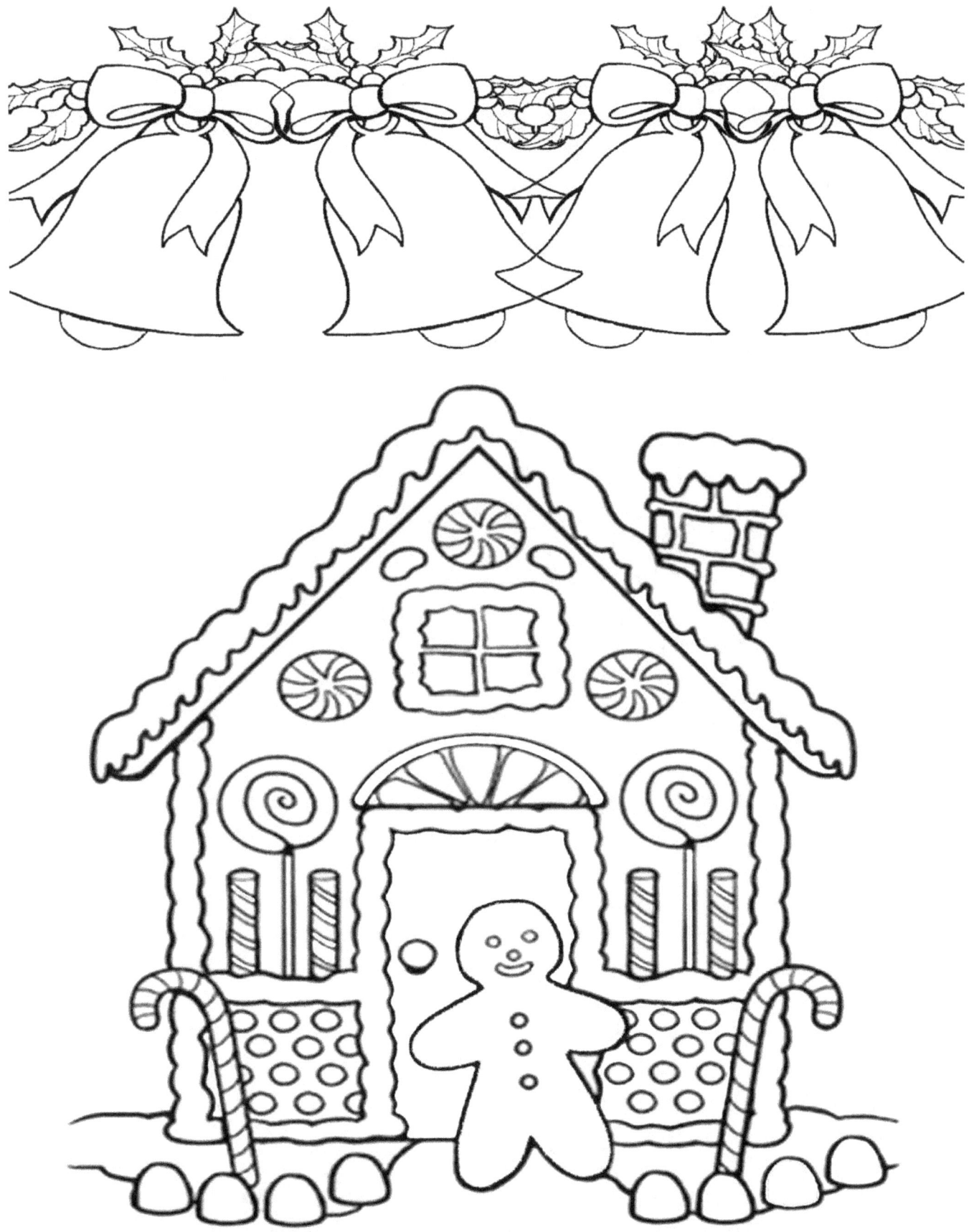

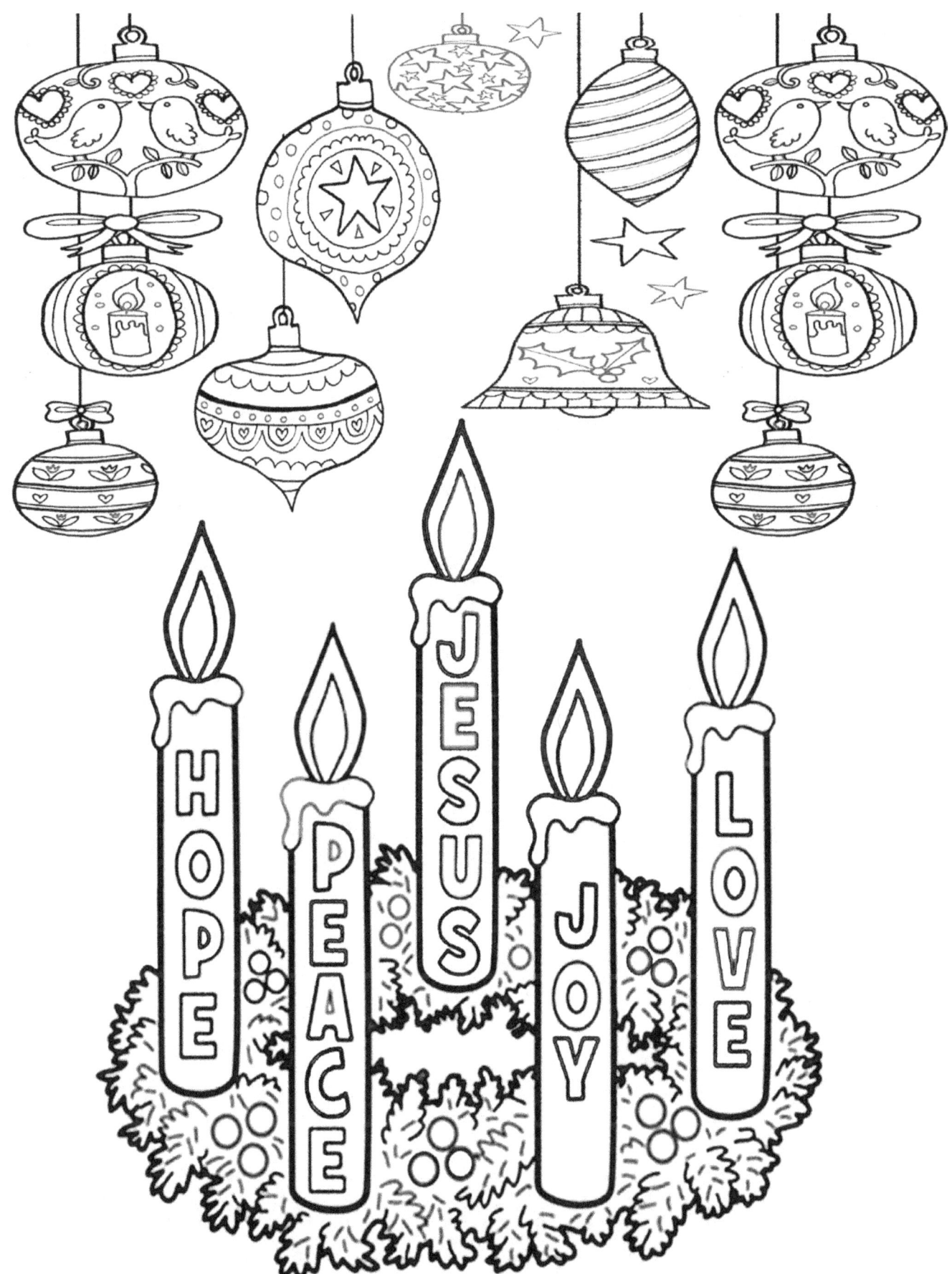

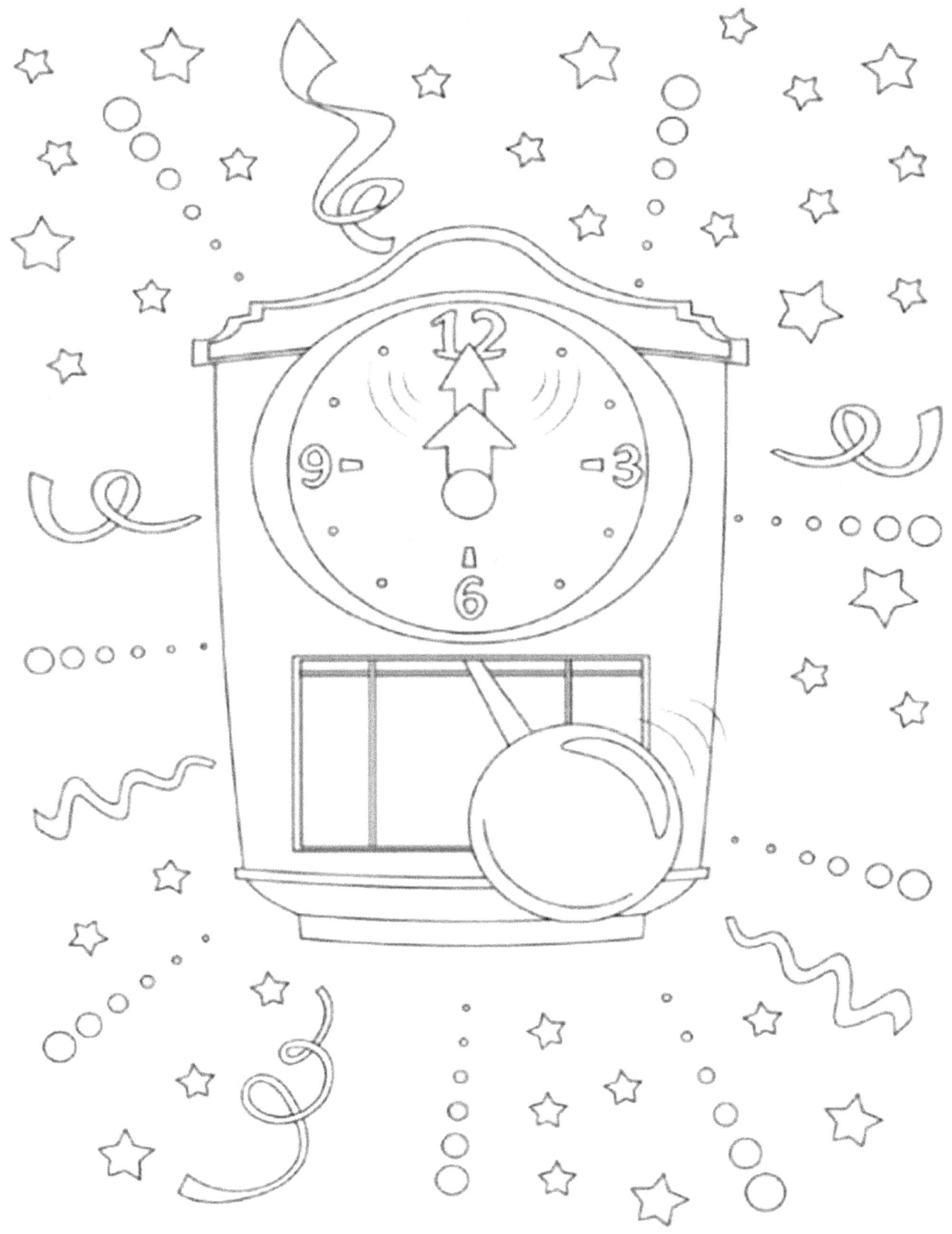

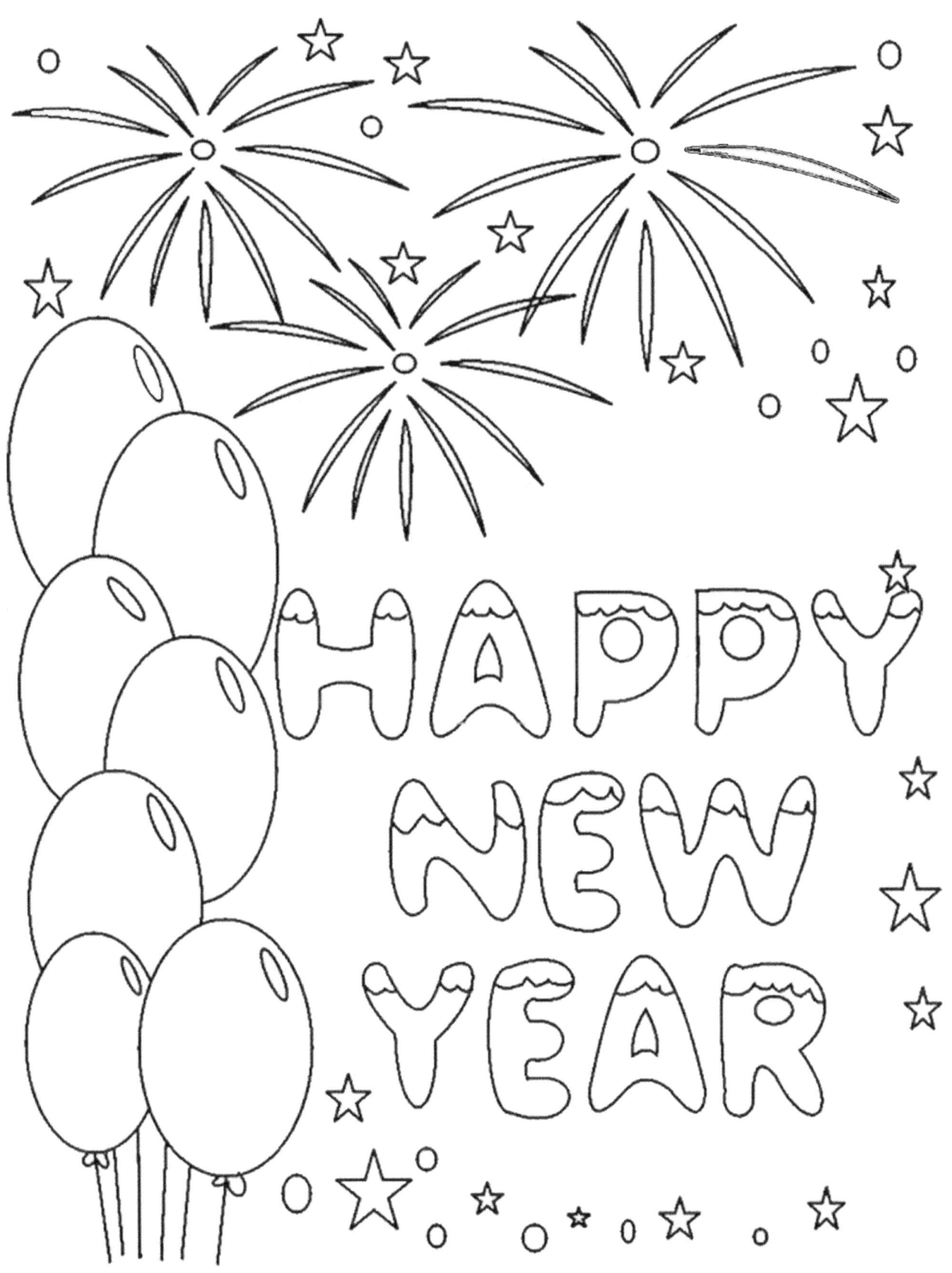

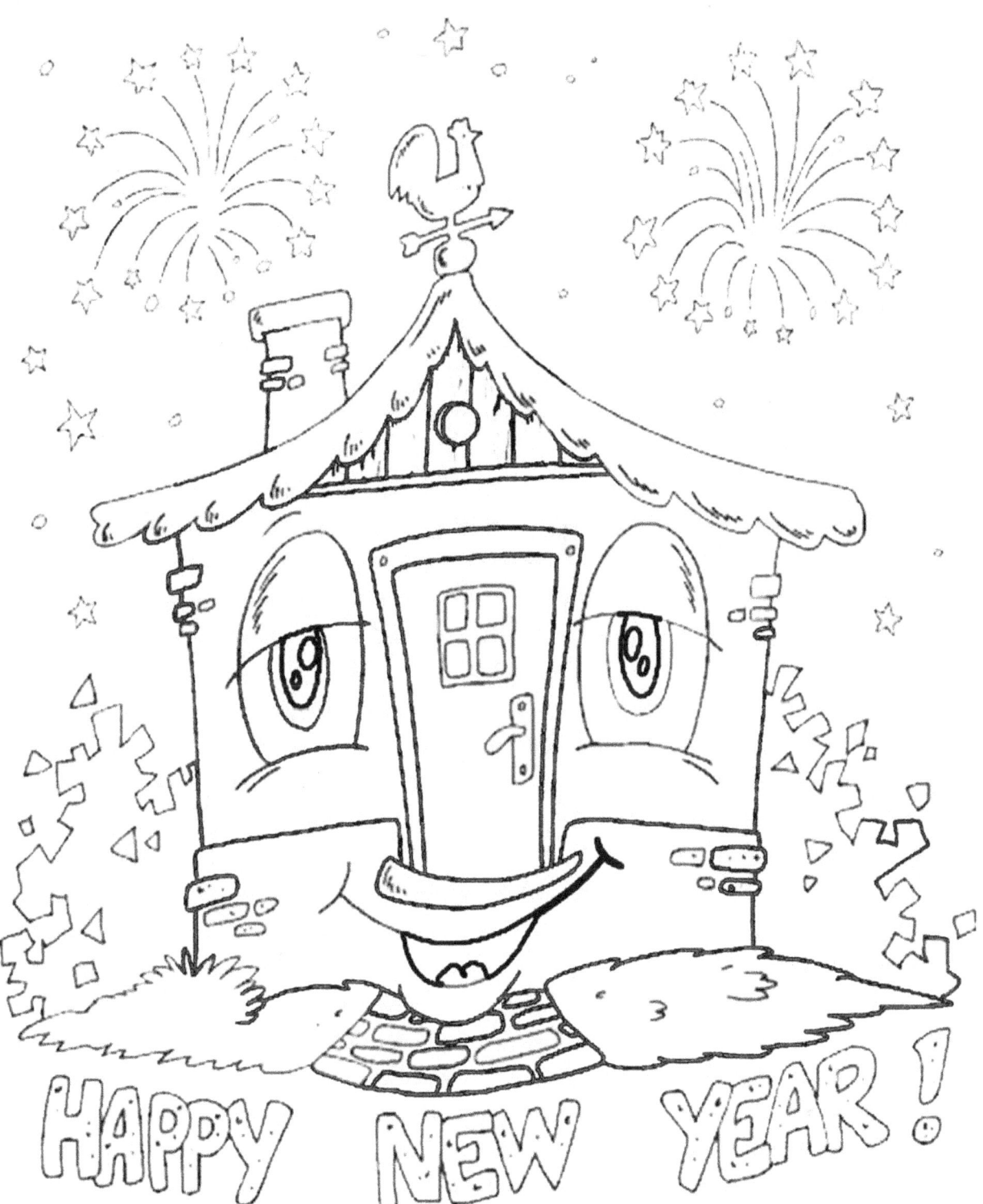

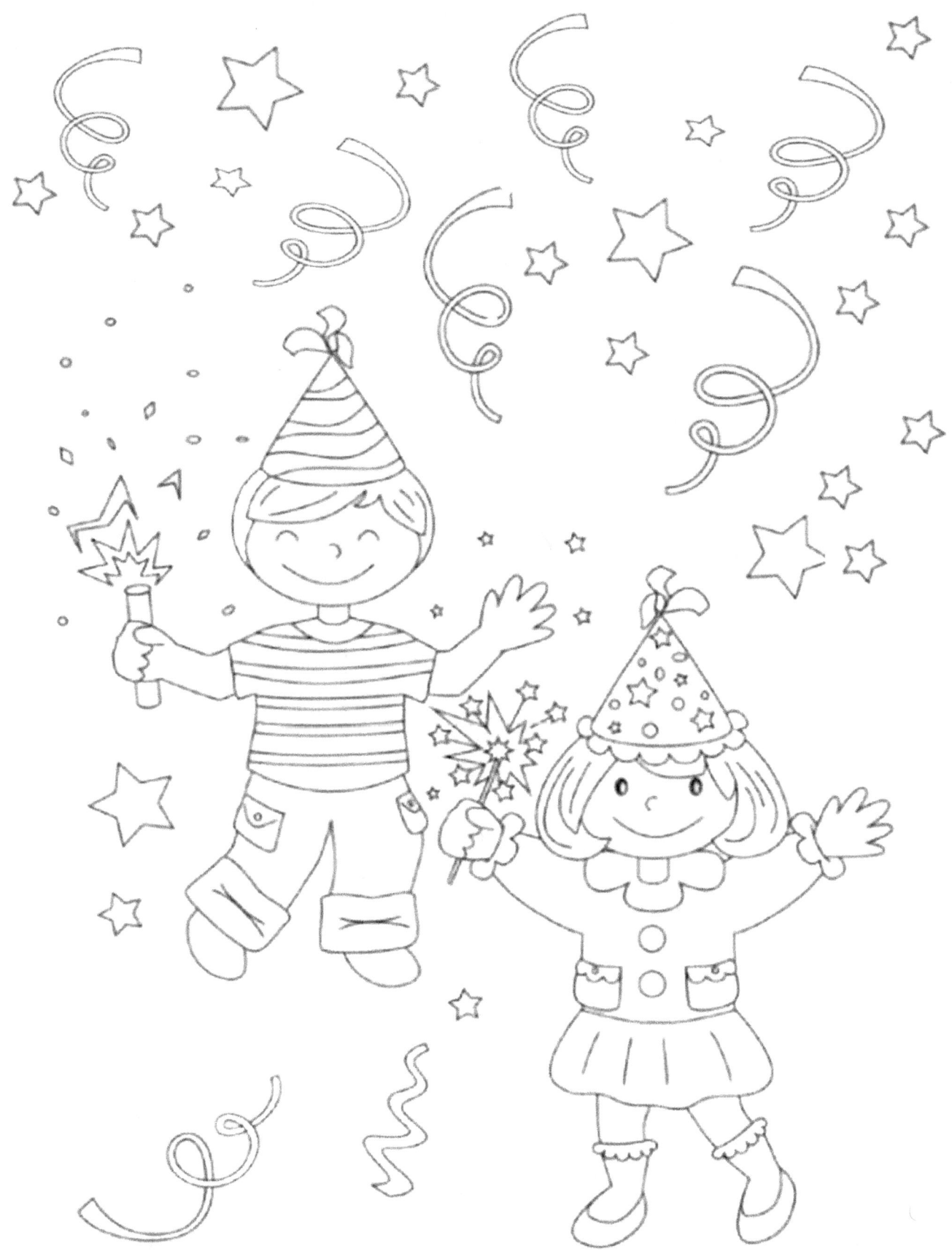

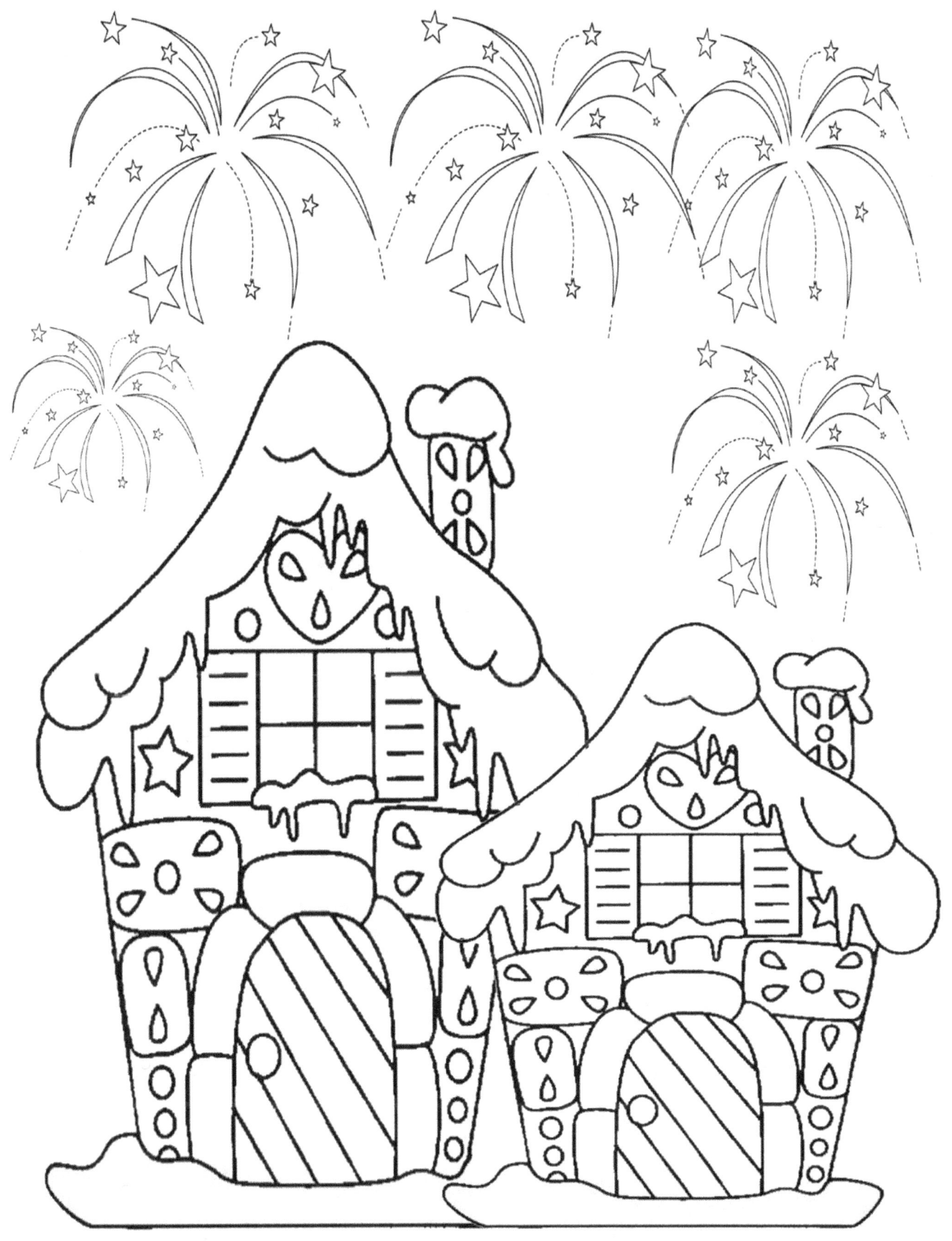

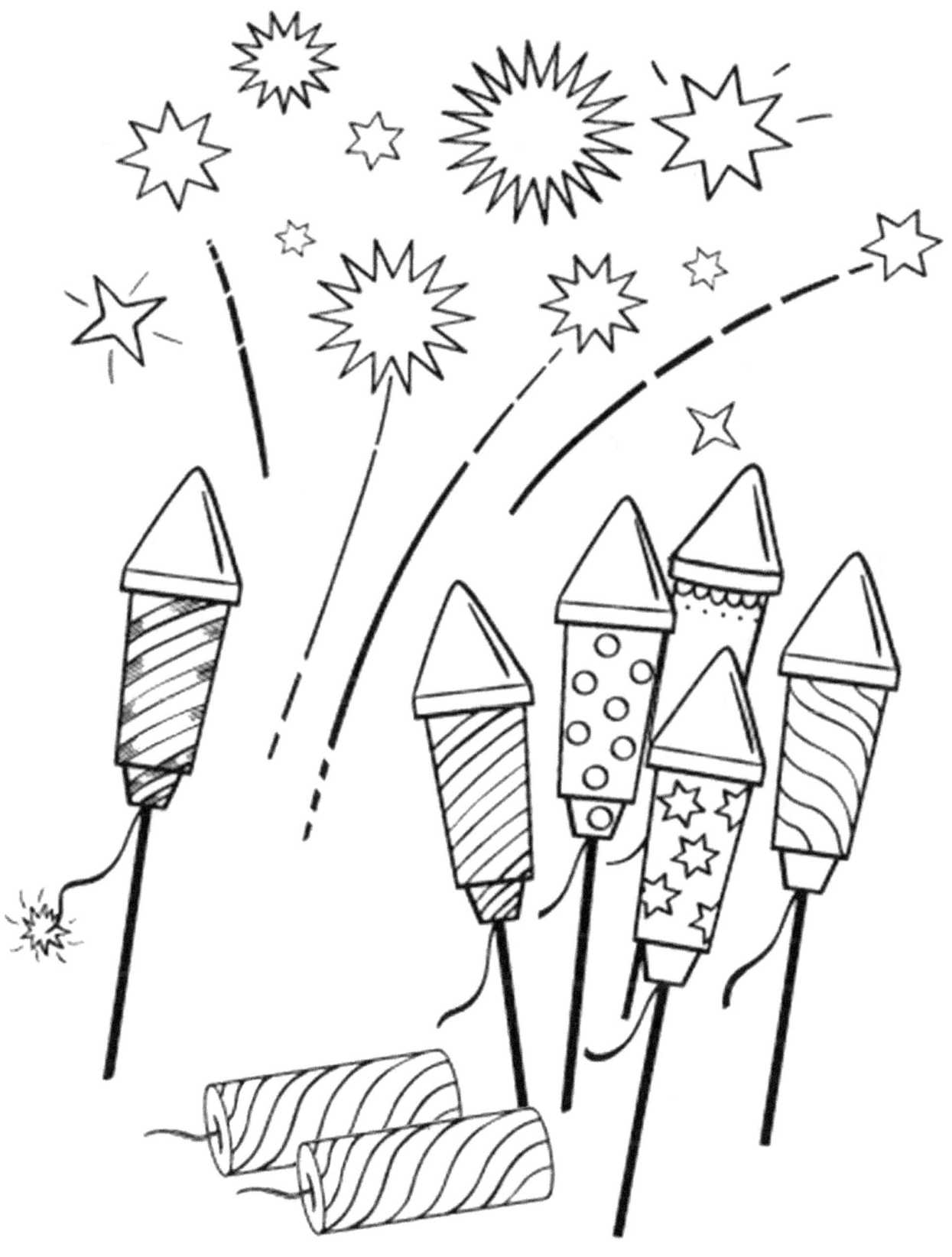

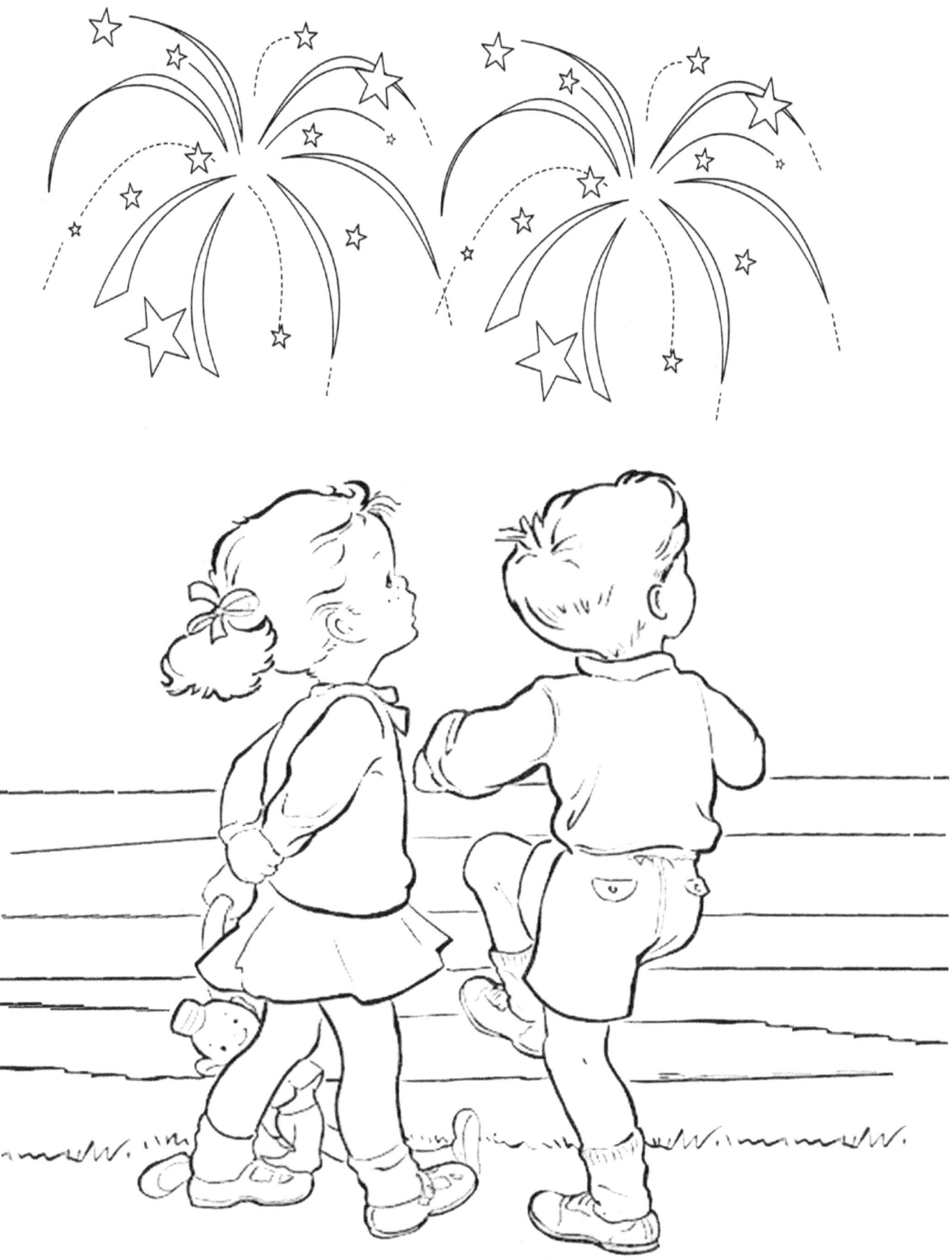

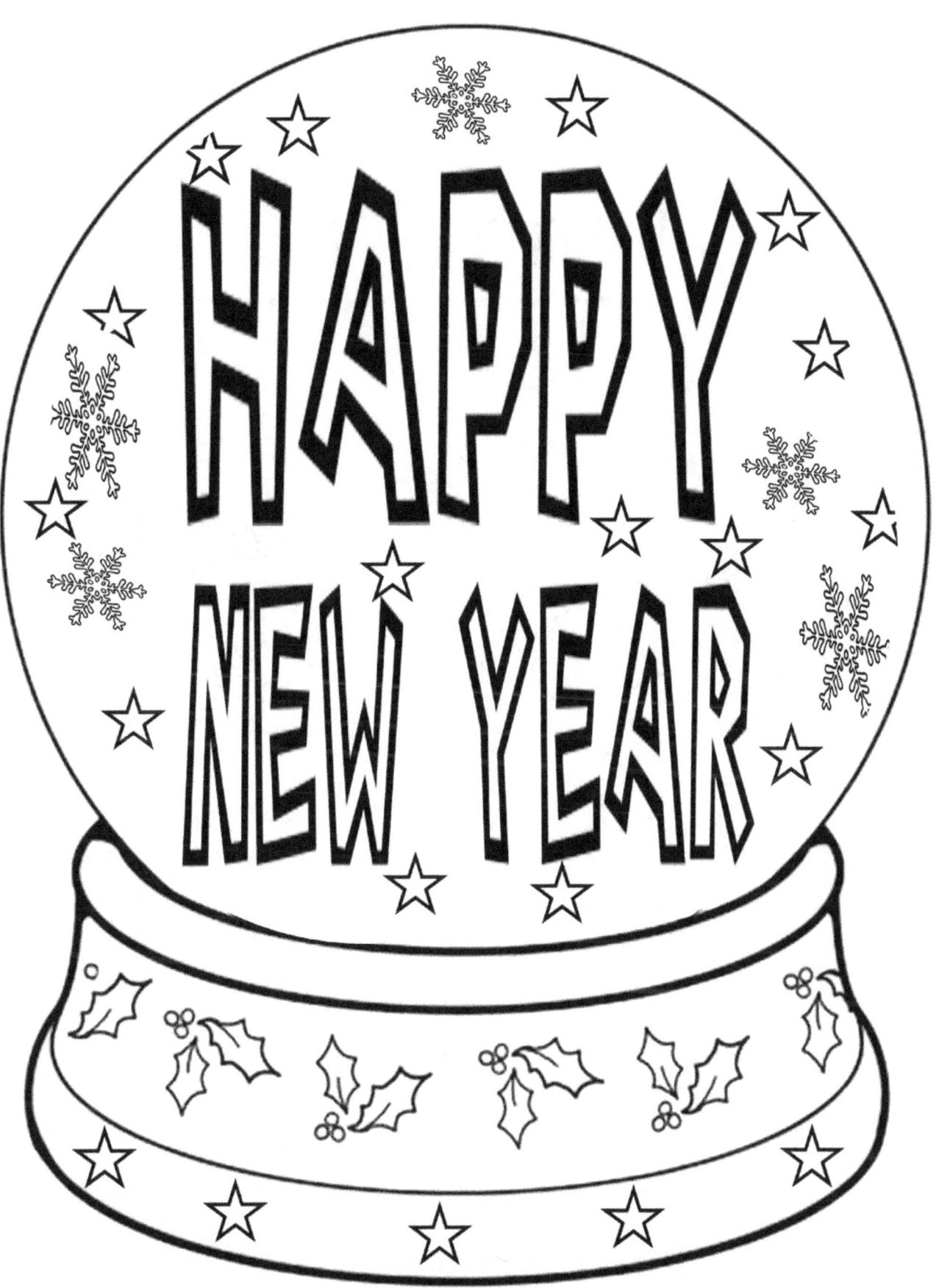

ThankYou

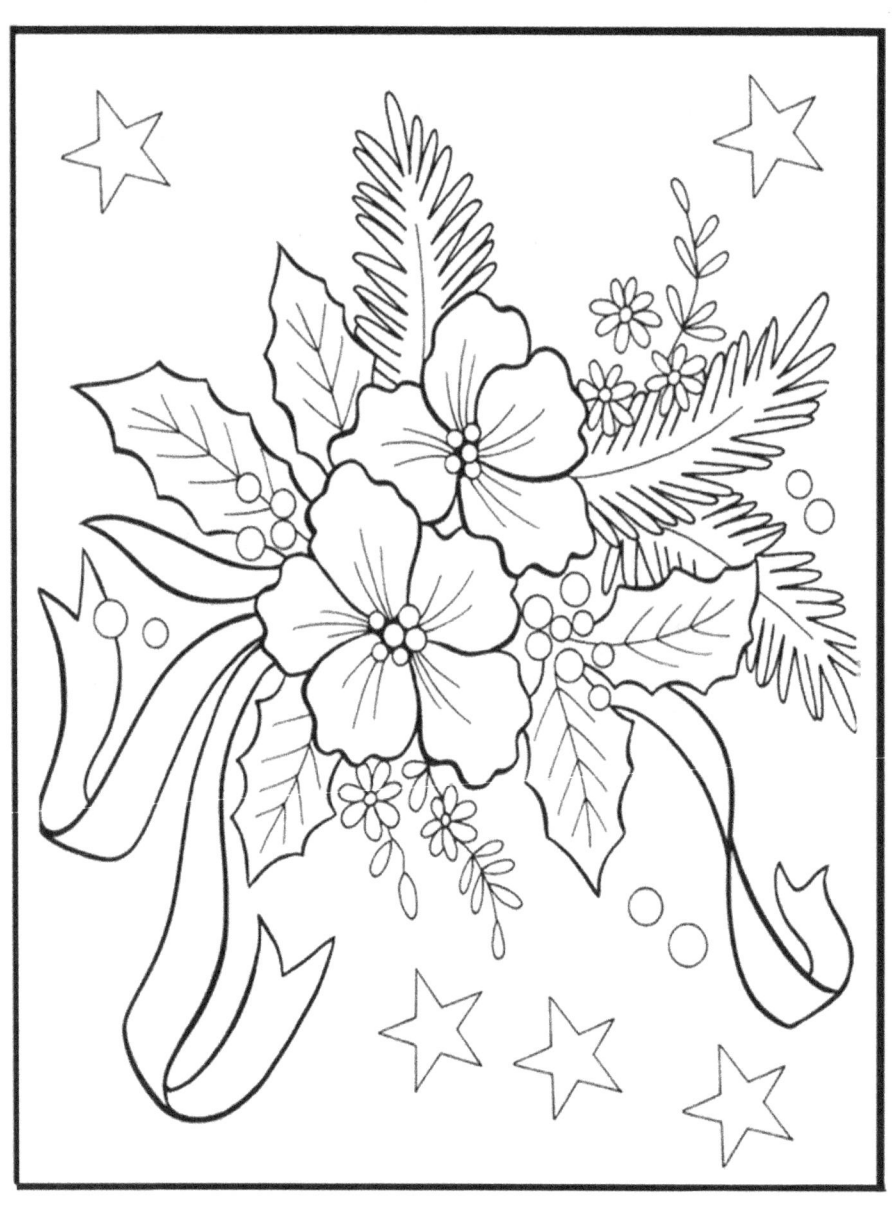

www.ingramcontent.com/pod-product-compliance
Lightning Source LLC
Chambersburg PA
CBHW082214220526
45470CB00010B/3163